WHAT IS A
HEALTHY CHURCH?

WHAT IS A HEALTHY CHURCH?

MARK DEVER

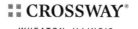

:: CROSSWAY®

WHEATON, ILLINOIS

What Is a Healthy Church?

Copyright © 2005, 2007 by Mark E. Dever and 9Marks

Published by Crossway
        1300 Crescent Street
        Wheaton, Illinois 60187

What Is a Healthy Church? © 2007 is a fifth edition; the fourth edition was *Nine Marks of a Healthy Church* © 2005 Mark E. Dever. *What Is a Healthy Church?* is not an abridged edition of *9 Marks of a Healthy Church* © 2000, 2004 by Mark Dever.

Cover design: Josh Dennis

Cover photo: iStock

Printed in the United States of America

ISBN-13: 978-1-58134-106-5
ISBN-10: 1-58134-106-7
ePub ISBN: 978-1-4335-4073-8
PDF ISBN: 978-1-4335-4063-9
Mobipocket ISBN: 978-1-4335-4064-6

Library of Congress Cataloging-in-Publication Data
Dever, Mark.
   What is a healthy church? / Mark Dever.
      p.   cm.
   "Adapted from 9 marks of a healthy church, © 2005 by Mark Dever"—T.p. verso.
   ISBN 13: 978-1-58134-937-5 (hc)
   1. Church—Marks. 2. Church—Biblical teaching. 3. Choice of church. I. Dever, Mark. 9 marks of a healthy church. II. Title.
BV601.D49   2007
250—dc22   2006102865

Crossway is a publishing ministry of Good News Publishers.

LB			24	23	22	21	20	19	18	17	16
23	22	21	20	19	18	17	16	15	14		

CONTENTS

PREFACE: A PARABLE

God has arranged the parts in the body, every one of them, just as he wanted them to be. If they were all one part, where would the body be? As it is, there are many parts but one body. The eye cannot say to the hand, "I don't need you!" And the head cannot say to the feet, "I don't need you!"

—1 CORINTHIANS 12:18–21

Nose and Hand were sitting in the church pew talking. The morning service, led by Ear and Mouth, had just ended, and Hand was telling Nose that he and his family had decided to look for a different church.

"Really?" Nose responded to Hand's news. "Why?"

"Oh, I don't know," Hand said, looking down. He was usually slower to speak than other members of the church body. "I guess because the church doesn't have what Mrs. Hand and I are looking for."

"Well, what are you looking for in a church?" Nose asked. The tone in which he spoke these words was sympathetic. But even as he was speaking them he knew he would dismiss Hand's answer. If the Hands couldn't see that Nose and the rest of the leadership were pointing the church body in the right direction, the body could do without them.

Hand had to think before answering. He and Mrs. Hand liked Pastor Mouth and his family. And Minister of Music Ear meant well. "Well, I guess we're looking for a place where people are more like us," Hand finally stammered. "We tried spending time with the Legs, but we didn't connect with them. Next we joined the small group for all the Toes. But they kept talking about socks and shoes and odors. And that didn't interest us."

Nose looked at him this time with genuine dismay: "Aren't you glad they're concerned with odors?!"

"Sure, sure. But it's not for us. Then, we attended the Sunday school for all you facial features. Do you remember? We came for several Sundays a couple of months ago?"

"It was great to have you."

"Thank you. But everyone just wanted to talk, and listen, and smell, and taste. It felt like, well, it felt like you never wanted to get to work and get your hands dirty. Anyway, Mrs. Hand and I were thinking about checking out that new church over on East Side. We hear they do a lot of clapping and hand-raising, which is closer to what we need right now."

"Hmmm," Nose replied. "I see what you mean. We'd hate to see you go. But I guess you have to do what's good for you."

At that moment, Mrs. Hand, who had been caught up in another conversation, turned back to join her husband and Nose. Hand briefly explained what he and Nose had been talking about, after which Nose repeated his sadness at the prospect of losing the Hands. But he again said that he understood since it sounded like their needs weren't being met.

Mrs. Hand nodded in agreement. She wanted to be polite,

but, truth be told, she wasn't sad to be leaving. Her husband had made just enough critical remarks about the church over the years that her heart had begun to reflect his. No, he had never burst into an open tirade against the body. In fact, he usually apologized for "being so negative," as he put it. But the little complaints that he let slip out here and there had had an effect. The small groups *were* a little cliquish. The music *was* a little out of date. The programs *did* seem a little silly. The teaching *wasn't* entirely to their liking. In the end, it was hard for the two of them to put their fingers on it, but they finally decided that the church wasn't for them.

In addition to all that, Mrs. Hand knew that their daughter Pinkie was not comfortable with the youth group. Everyone was so different from her, she felt out of joint.

Mrs. Hand then said something about how much she appreciated Nose and the leadership. But the conversation had already run on too long for Nose. Besides, her perfume made him want to sneeze. He thanked Mrs. Hand for her encouragement, repeated that he was sorry to hear of their departure, then turned and walked away. Who needed the Hands? Apparently, they didn't need him.

INTRODUCTION:
WHAT ARE YOU LOOKING FOR
IN A CHURCH?

So what are you looking for in a church? You might not have thought about that question lately. But take a moment now to ask yourself, what does the ideal church look like? "The ideal church is a place with . . ."

Beautiful music—music that shows training and practice. You don't want guitars and drums. You want a choir and violin players. Beautiful music glorifies God. Or maybe you do want guitars and drums, something contemporary and up-to-date. That's what people listen to on the radio, so meet them where they are.

Maybe the music is not as important to you as the preaching. You want a church where the sermons are good—meaningful, but not heavy-handed, biblical, but not boring, practical, but not picky and legalistic. Of course, the kind of man the preacher is plays into what his sermons are like, and there are all kinds of preachers out there: the intense scholar who loves doctrine and never smiles, the funny guy with a million stories, the family counselor who has "been there." Yes, I'm just caricaturing, but most of us do have some expectations of what a pastor should be like, don't we?

Or perhaps you're looking for a church where the people are at the same place in life as you are. You can connect with them. They understand what you're going through because they're going through the same. They're just out of college like you. They have young children like you. They are nearing retirement like you. They know what it's like to shop at thrift stores like you, or designer boutiques like you. They are from the inner city like you, or maybe it's the country.

Then again, maybe the most important thing for you about a church is whether or not there are opportunities to get involved—places to serve, places to do good. Is the church big on evangelism? Is it big on missions? Is it big on helping the poor? Does it provide opportunities for you and your son to meet with other fathers and sons? What about opportunities for you to help out in the children's ministry? Does it have programs that hold the attention of your kids or teens?

I expect that some people are looking for a church that is "alive to the Spirit." The Spirit is the one who guides us, so you want a church where people are quick to listen to his voice, quick to watch for his work, quick to believe the remarkable things he can do. You're tired of being around Spirit-quenchers and tradition-lovers. The Spirit's doing new things! He's giving us new songs!

Or maybe you're just looking for a church that feels a certain way. Not that you've ever put it like that. But if you are used to a church that feels kind of like a mall, or an old chapel, or a coffee house, it makes sense that your ideal church feels the same. That's to be expected. Didn't many of us, when we moved away from our parents' home, occasionally find

ourselves nostalgic for certain sights, smells, or sounds of the
way mom or dad did things?

A lot of these things can be good, or at least neutral.
Really, I just want you to start thinking about what you value
most in a church.

What are you looking for? A place that's welcoming?
Passionate? Authentic? Big? Intimate? Trendy? Exciting? Hard
core?

What should a church be?

A Topic for All Christians

Before we consider what the Bible says churches should be,
which we will do in the first few chapters, I want you to consider why I would pose this question to *you*, especially if you
are not a pastor. After all, isn't a book on the topic of healthy
churches a book for pastors and church leaders?

It is for pastors, yes, but it's also for every Christian.
Remember: *that's who the authors of the New Testament
address.* When the churches in Galatia began listening to false
teachers, Paul wrote to them and said, "I am astonished that
you are so quickly deserting the one who called you by the
grace of Christ" (Gal. 1:6). Who was the "you" that Paul
called to account for the false teaching in their churches? Not
the pastors alone but the church bodies themselves. You'd
expect him to write to the churches' leaders and say, "Stop
teaching that heresy!" But he doesn't. He calls the whole
church to account.

Likewise, when the church in the city of Corinth allowed for
an adulterous relationship to continue unchecked in their midst,
Paul again directly addressed the church (1 Corinthians 5). He

didn't tell the pastors or the staff to take care of the problem. He told the church to take care of it.

So it is with the majority of letters in the New Testament.

I trust the pastors of those first-century churches were listening as Paul and Peter, James and John, addressed their congregations. And I trust the pastors initiated and led the way in responding to whatever instructions the apostles gave in their letters. Yet by following the apostles' example and addressing *you*, pastor and members alike, I believe I'm placing responsibility where, humanly, it ultimately belongs. *You* and all the members of your church, Christian, are finally responsible before God for what your church becomes, not your pastors and other leaders—*you*.

Your pastors will stand before God and give an account for how they have led your congregation (Heb. 13:17). But every single one of us who is a disciple of the Lord Jesus Christ will give an account for whether or not we have *gathered* together regularly with the church, *spurred* the church on to love and good deeds, and *fought* to maintain a right teaching of the hope of the gospel (Heb. 10:23–25).

Friend, if you call yourself a Christian but you think a book about healthy churches is a book for church leaders or maybe for those "theological types," while you would rather read books about the Christian life, it may be time to stop and consider again exactly what the Bible says a Christian is. We'll think more about that in chapter 1.

Following that, we'll consider what the church is (chapter 2), what God's ultimate purpose for churches is (chapter 3), and why the Bible must guide our churches (chapter 4).

If you already agree that the Bible should guide our

churches for the display of God's glory, you may want to jump straight to chapter 5, where I begin listing nine marks of a healthy church. May he use our meditations together to prepare his bride for the day of his coming (Eph. 5:25–32).

PART 1

WHAT IS A HEALTHY CHURCH?

CHAPTER ONE

YOUR CHRISTIANITY AND YOUR CHURCH

Sometimes college campus ministries will ask me to speak to their students. I've been known, on several occasions, to begin my remarks this way: "If you call yourself a Christian but you are not a member of the church you regularly attend, I worry that you might be going to hell."

You could say that it gets their attention.

Now, am I just going for shock value? I don't think so. Am I trying to scare them into church membership? Not really. Am I saying that joining a church makes someone a Christian? Certainly not! Throw any book (or speaker) out the window that says as much.

So why would I begin with this kind of warning? It's because I want them to see something of the urgency of the need for a healthy local church in the Christian's life and to begin sharing the passion for the church that characterizes both Christ and his followers.

Many Christians in the West today (and elsewhere?) tend to view their Christianity as a personal relationship with God and not much else. They generally know that this "personal relationship" has some implications for how they should live. But I'm concerned that many Christians don't realize how this most important relationship with God necessitates a number of secondary personal relationships—the relationships that Christ establishes between us and his body, the Church. God doesn't mean for these to be relationships that we pick and choose at our whim among the many Christians "out there." He means to establish us in relationship with an actual flesh-and-blood, step-on-your-toes body of people.

Why do I worry that if you call yourself a Christian but you are not a member in good standing of the local church you attend, you might be going to hell? Think with me for a moment about what a Christian is.

What a Christian Is

A Christian is someone who, first and foremost, has been forgiven of his sin and been reconciled to God the Father through Jesus Christ. This happens when a person repents of his sins and puts his faith in the perfect life, substitutionary death, and resurrection of Jesus Christ, the Son of God.

In other words, a Christian is someone who has reached the end of himself and his own moral resources. He has recognized that he, in defiance of God's plainly revealed law, has given his life over to worshiping and loving things other than God—things like career, family, the stuff money can buy, the opinions of other people, the honor of his family and community, the favor of the so-called gods of other religions, the spirits of this world, or even the good things a person can do. He has also recognized that these "idols" are doubly damning masters. Their appetites are never satisfied in *this life*. And they provoke God's just wrath over *the next life*, a death and a judgment the Christian has already tasted a bit of (mercifully) in this world's miseries.

A Christian, therefore, knows that if he were to die tonight and stand before God, and if God were to say, "Why should I let you into my presence?" the Christian would say, "You shouldn't let me in. I have sinned and owe you a debt that I cannot pay back." But he wouldn't stop there. He would continue, "Yet, because of your great promises and mercy, I depend on the blood of Jesus Christ shed as a substitute for me, paying my moral debt, satisfying your holy and righteous requirements, and removing your wrath against sin!"

Upon that plea to be declared righteous in Christ, the Christian is someone who has discovered the beginning of freedom from sin's enslavement. Where the idols and other gods could never be satisfied, their stomachs never full, God's satisfaction in the work of Christ means that the person purchased out of condemnation by Christ's work is now free! For the first time ever, the Christian is free to turn his back on sin, not just to replace it slavishly with yet another sin but with the Holy Spirit–given desire for Jesus Christ himself and for Christ's rule in his life. Where Adam tried to push God off the throne and make himself god, the Christian rejoices that Christ is upon the throne. He considers Jesus' life of perfect submission to the will and words of the Father and seeks to be like his Savior.

So a Christian is someone who, first of all, has been reconciled to God in Christ. Christ has assuaged the wrath of

God, and the Christian is now declared righteous before God, called to a life of righteousness, and lives in the hope of one day appearing before his majesty in heaven.

Yet that's not all! Second, a Christian is someone who, by virtue of his reconciliation with God, has been reconciled to God's people. Do you remember the first story in the Bible after Adam and Eve's fall and banishment from the garden? It's the story of one human being murdering another—Cain killing Abel. If the act of trying to shove God off the throne is, by its very nature, an act of trying to place ourselves upon it, we're not about to let some other human being take it from us. Not a chance. Adam's act of breaking fellowship with God resulted in an immediate break in fellowship among all human beings. It's every man for himself.

It should be no surprise, then, that Jesus said that "all the Law and the Prophets hang on these two commandments": love the Lord your God with all your heart, soul, and mind *and* love your neighbor as yourself (see Matt. 22:34–40). The two commandments go together. The first produces the second, and the second proves the first.

Through Christ, then, being reconciled to God means being reconciled to everyone else who is reconciled to God. After describing in the first half of Ephesians 2 the great salvation that God has given us in Christ Jesus, Paul turns, in the second half of Ephesians 2, to describing what this means for the relationship between Jews and Gentiles and, by extension, between all those who are in Christ. He writes:

> For he himself is our peace, who has made the two one and has destroyed the barrier, the dividing wall of hostility. . . . His purpose was to create in himself one new man out of the two,

thus making peace, and in this one body to reconcile both of them to God through the cross, by which he put to death their hostility. (Eph. 2:14–16)

Now, all those who belong to God are "fellow citizens" and "members of God's household" (v. 19). We are "joined together" with Christ into one "holy temple" (v. 21)—so many rich analogies to choose from!

A Family, a Fellowship, and a Body

Perhaps meditating on the analogy of a household will help us see that being reconciled to God also means being reconciled to his people. If you're an orphan, you don't adopt parents; they adopt you. If your adoptive parents are named Smith, you now attend the Smith family dinners with the parents and all the children. You share a bedroom at night with the Smith siblings. When the teacher at school calls out attendance and says, "Smith?" you raise your hand like your older brother did before you and your younger sister will do after you. And you do this not because you decided to play the role of "Smith," but because someone went to the orphanage and said, "You will be a Smith." On that day, you became the child of someone and the sibling of others.

Only your name's not Smith. It's *Christ*ian, named after the one through whom you were adopted, Christ (Eph. 1:5). Now you're part of the whole family of God. "The one who makes men holy and those who are made holy are of the same family" (Heb. 2:11).

And this is no dysfunctional family, with family members estranged from one another. It's a fellowship. When God "called you into fellowship with his Son Jesus Christ our Lord" (1 Cor. 1:9), he also called you into "fellowship" with the whole family (1 Cor. 5:2).

And this is no polite and formal fellowship. It's a body, bound together by our individual decisions but also bound together by far more than human decision—the person and work of Christ. You would be as foolish to say, "I'm not a part of the family," as you would be to cut off your own hand or nose. As Paul said to the Corinthians, "The eye cannot say to the hand, 'I don't need you!' And the head cannot say to the feet, 'I don't need you!'" (1 Cor. 12:21).

In short, it's impossible to answer the question *what is a Christian?* without ending up in a conversation about the church; at least, in the Bible it is. Not only that, it's hard to stick with just one metaphor for the church because the New Testament uses so many of them: a family and a fellowship, a body and a bride, a people and a temple, a lady and her children. And never does the New Testament conceive of the Christian existing on a prolonged basis *outside* the fellowship of the church. The church is not really a place. It's a people— God's people in Christ.

Joining an Actual Church

When a person becomes a Christian, he doesn't just join a local church because it's a good habit for growing in spiritual maturity. He joins a local church because it's the expression of what Christ has *made him*—a member of the body of Christ. Being united to Christ means being united to every Christian. But that universal union must be given a living, breathing existence in a local church.

Sometimes theologians refer to a distinction between the universal church (all Christians everywhere throughout history) and the local church (those people who meet down the street from you to hear the Word preached and to practice baptism and the Lord's Supper). Other than a few references to the universal church (such as Matt. 16:18 and the bulk of Ephesians), most references to the church in the New Testament are to local churches, as when Paul writes, "To the church of God in Corinth" or "To the churches in Galatia."

Now what follows is a little intense, but it's important. The relationship between our *membership in the universal church* and our *membership in the local church* is a lot like the relationship between *the righteousness God gives us through faith* and the *actual practice of righteousness in our daily lives.* When we become Christians by faith, God declares us righteous. Yet we are still called to actively *be* righteous. A person who happily goes on living in unrighteousness calls into question whether he ever possessed Christ's righteousness in the first place (see Rom. 6:1–18; 8:5–14; James 2:14–15). So, too, it is with those who refuse to commit themselves to a local church. Committing to a local body is the natural outcome—it confirms what Christ has done. If you have no interest in actually committing yourself to an actual group of gospel-believing, Bible-teaching Christians, you might question whether you belong to the body of Christ at all! Listen to the author of Hebrews carefully:

> Let us hold unswervingly to the hope we profess, for he who promised is faithful. And let us consider how we may spur one another on toward love and good deeds. Let us not give up meeting together, as some are in the habit of doing, but let us

encourage one another—and all the more as you see the Day
approaching. If we deliberately keep on sinning after we have
received the knowledge of the truth, no sacrifice for sins is left,
but only a fearful expectation of judgment and of raging fire that
will consume the enemies of God. (Heb. 10:23–27)

Our state before God, if authentic, will translate into our
daily decisions, even if the process is slow and full of missteps.
God really does change his people. Isn't that good news? So
please, friend, don't grow complacent through some vague
idea that you possess the righteousness of Christ if you're
not pursuing a life of righteousness. Likewise, please do not
be deceived by a vague conception of the universal church to
which you belong if you're not pursuing that life together with
an actual church.

Except for the rarest of circumstances, a true Christian
builds his life into the lives of other believers through the concrete fellowship of a local church. He knows he has not yet
"arrived." He's still fallen and needs the accountability and
instruction of that local body of people called the church. And
they need him.

As we gather to worship God and exercise love and good
deeds toward one another, we demonstrate in real life, you
might say, the fact that God has reconciled us to himself and to
one another. We demonstrate to the world that we have been
changed, not primarily because we memorize Bible verses,
pray before meals, tithe a portion of our income, and listen to
Christian radio stations, but because we increasingly show a
willingness to put up with, to forgive, and even to love a bunch
of fellow sinners.

You and I cannot demonstrate love or joy or peace or

patience or kindness sitting all by ourselves on an island. No, we demonstrate it when the people we have committed to loving give us good reasons *not* to love them, but we do anyway.

Do you see it? It's right there—right in the midst of a group of sinners who have committed to loving one another—that the gospel is displayed. The church gives a visual presentation of the gospel when we forgive one another as Christ has forgiven us, when we commit to one another as Christ has committed to us, and when we lay down our lives for one another as Christ laid down his life for us.

Together we can display the gospel of Jesus Christ in a way we just can't by ourselves.

I often hear Christians talking about their different spiritual gifts. Yet I wonder how often people consider the fact that God has given so many gifts precisely so that those gifts might be used in response to the sin of other Christians in the church. My sins give you a chance to exercise your gifts.

So gather up a group of men and women, young and old, black and white, Asian and African, rich and poor, uneducated and educated, with all their diverse talents and gifts and offerings. Just make sure *all of them* know they're sick, sinful, and saved by grace alone. What do you have? You have the makings for a church!

If your goal is to love *all* Christians, let me suggest working toward it by first committing to a concrete group of *real* Christians with all their foibles and follies. Commit to them through thick and thin for eighty years. Then come back and we'll talk about your progress in loving all Christians everywhere.

Giving an Account

So who's responsible for thinking about what the gathering of people called the church should be like? Is it pastors and church leaders? Definitely. How about every other Christian? Absolutely. Being a Christian means caring about the life and health of the body of Christ, the church. It means caring about what the church is and what the church should be because you belong to the church, Christian.

Indeed, we care for the church because it's the very body of our Savior. Have you noticed the words that Jesus used with the Christian-persecuting Saul—soon to be called Paul—when he confronted Saul on the road to Damascus? "Saul, Saul, why do you persecute *me*?" (Acts 9:4). Jesus identifies so closely with his church that he refers to it as himself! Christian, do you identify yourself with those whom your Savior identifies himself? Does your heart share the passions of his heart?

A letter was forwarded to me not long ago from a pastor who expressed in the letter his desire for the members of his church to know what a church should be. This humble man wants a church that would help hold him accountable as he leads them toward grace and godliness. This pastor understands the New Testament pattern. He understands that one day, God will call him to account for how he has shepherded his congregation. And, like a faithful shepherd, he wants every sheep in his flock to know that, one day, they too will be called one by one to account for how they have loved one another and him.

God will ask each member of the body, "Did you rejoice with the other members of the body when they rejoiced? Did you mourn with those who mourned? Did you treat the weaker parts as indispensable, and did you treat the parts that most think less honorable with special honor? Did you give double honor to those that led and taught you?" (see 1 Cor. 12:22–26 and 1 Tim. 5:17).

Christian, are you ready for the day on which God will call you to account for how you have loved and served the church family, including your church leaders? Do you know what God says the church should be?

And pastor, have you been preparing your flock for their account-giving by teaching them what the church should be? Have you taught them that they will be held accountable for whether or not you hold fast to the gospel?

CHAPTER TWO

WHAT A CHURCH IS . . . AND ISN'T

In the introduction I asked what you are looking for in a church as well as what the Bible says the church should be, but I never answered these questions. No doubt these are tough questions. And Christians today are looking for all sorts of different things in a church.

A Jarring Conversation

During my graduate studies, I remember one conversation with a friend who worked for a Christian ministry that was not affiliated with any one church. He and I did attend the same church for a couple of years. But while I joined the church as a member, my friend didn't. In fact, he only came for the Sunday morning service and would slip in about halfway through, just in time for the sermon.

One day, I decided to ask him about his halfhearted attendance. "I don't really get anything out of the rest of the service," he replied.

"Have you ever thought of joining the church?" I asked.

He appeared genuinely surprised by my question and responded, "Join the church? I honestly don't know why I would do that. I know what I'm here for, and those people would just slow me down."

As far as I could tell, he didn't say those words disdainfully, but with the genuine zeal of a gifted evangelist who did not want to waste one hour of the Lord's time. He had given some thought to what he was looking for in a church. And on the whole it didn't involve the other members of the church, at least not that church. He wanted a place where he could hear good preaching from God's Word and get his spiritual jolt for the week.

Yet his words reverberated in my mind—"those people would just slow me down." There were a number of things I wanted to say, but all I said was, "But did you ever think that if you linked arms with those people, yes, they may slow you down, but you may help to speed them up? Have you thought that might be a part of God's plan for them, and for you?"

I, too, wanted a church where I could hear good preaching every Sunday. But the words, "body of Christ," mean more than just that, don't they?

A People, Not a Place

As I mentioned in chapter 1, the church is not a place. It's not a building. It's not a preaching point. It's not a spiritual service provider. It's a people—the new covenant, blood-bought people of God. That's why Paul said, "Christ loved the church and gave himself up for her" (Eph. 5:25). He didn't give himself up for a place, but for a people.

That's why the church I pastor starts its Sunday morning

gatherings not by saying, "Welcome to Capitol Hill Baptist Church," but "Welcome to *this gathering* of the Capitol Hill Baptist Church." We are a people who gather. Yes, this is a small thing, but we're trying to point to a big reality even in the words we use to welcome people.

Remembering that the church is a people should help us recognize what's important and what's not important. I know I need the help. For example, I have a temptation to let something like the style of music dictate how I feel about a church. After all, the style of music a church uses is one of the first things we will notice about any church, and we tend to respond to music at a very emotional level. Music makes us *feel* a certain way. Yet what does it say about my love for Christ and for Christ's people if I decide to leave a church because of the style of its music? Or if, when pastoring a church, I marginalize a majority of my congregation because I think the style of music needs to be updated? At the very least, we could say that I've forgotten that the church, fundamentally, is a people and not a place.

At the same time, the Bible teaches that Christians should very much care about what happens at a church—what it *does*. In fact, the latter half of this book is devoted to such a discussion.

How do we balance these two things—caring about a people but also caring about what they do? If this were a book about raising Christian families, we would talk about *doing* certain things: eating dinner together, reading Scripture together, laughing together, praying for one another, and so on. Yet throughout the discussion, hopefully we would all remember that parents make mistakes and that kids will be kids. The family is not just an institution; it's a group of people.

So it is with a church. Does a particular church fail to meet your expectations in terms of what it *does,* as in whether or not it follows what the Bible says about church leadership (one topic that I'll cover later)? If so, remember that this is a group of people who are still growing in grace. Love them. Serve them. Be patient with them. Again, think of a family. Whenever your parents, siblings, or children fail to meet your expectations, do you suddenly throw them out of the family? I hope you forgive and are patient with them. You might even stop to consider whether it's your expectations that should be adjusted! By this same token, we should ask ourselves whether we know how to love and persevere with church members who have different opinions, who fail to meet expectations, or even who sin against us. (Don't you and I have sin that ever needs to be forgiven?)

Somewhere, of course, there is a line. There are some churches you may not want to join, or pastor, or remain joined to. We'll return to this question in the section on the essential marks of a church. For the time being, the basic principle remains the same: the church is a people. And whatever we're looking for, or whatever we're saying the church should be, must be guided by that basic, biblical principle.

A People, Not a Statistic

Let me put up one more road block to bad thinking about the church, thinking especially common among pastors. Not only is the church not a place, it's not a statistic.

When I was in graduate school, I remember encountering a letter of counsel written by John Brown, a pastor in the nineteenth century, to one of his students who had just been ordained over a small congregation. In the letter Brown wrote:

> I know the vanity of your heart, and that you will feel mortified that your congregation is very small, in comparison with those of your brethren around you; but assure yourself on the word of an old man, that when you come to give an account of them to the Lord Christ, at his judgment-seat, you will think you have had enough.[1]

As I considered the congregation over which God had given me charge, I felt the weightiness of this day of accounting before God. Did I want the church I pastored to become big? Popular and much discussed? A church that in some way looked impressive?

Was I motivated in any way to just "put up with" or "tolerate" the group of people in front of me, to bide my time and wait for opportunities to make the church into what I thought it should be? Not that having desires for a church's future is bad, but were my desires leading me to be indifferent, even annoyed, with the saints surrounding me in the present?

Or would I remember what was infinitely at stake for the several scores of souls, most of them elderly, already sitting in front of me on Sunday mornings in a room big enough for eight hundred? Would I love and serve these few, even if their unbiblical committees, and old-fashioned traditions, and not-my-favorite music selections stood in the way of my (I think

---

[1]James Hay and Henry Belfrage, *Memoir of the Rev. Alexander Waugh* (Edinburgh: William Oliphant and Son, 1839), 64–65.

legitimate) hopes for the church? And I know it's not only pastors who fall into "tolerating" the people around them, biding their time until the church becomes what they envision it can be.

The church is a people, not a place or a statistic. It's a body, united into him who is the head. It's a family, joined together by adoption through Christ.

I pray that we pastors would increasingly recognize our awesome responsibility for the particular flocks over which God has made us under-shepherds.

But I also pray that you, Christian, whether an elder or an infant in the faith, would increasingly recognize your responsibility to love, serve, encourage, and hold accountable the rest of your church family. When it comes to your flesh-and-blood siblings, I trust that you already recognize where Cain went wrong when he dismissively said to the Lord, "Am I my brother's keeper?" But even more I hope that you recognize, if you haven't already, your higher responsibility to the brothers and sisters of your church family.

> A crowd was sitting around [Jesus], and they told him, "Your mother and brothers are outside looking for you."
>
> "Who are my mother and my brothers?" he asked. Then he looked at those seated in a circle around him and said, "Here are my mother and my brothers! Whoever does God's will is my brother and sister and mother." (Mark 3:32–35)

CHAPTER THREE

WHAT EVERY CHURCH SHOULD ASPIRE TO BE: HEALTHY

If you're a Christian parent, what do you want for your kids? If you're a Christian kid, what do you want for your family?

Probably you want a number of attributes to increasingly mark your family: love, joy, holiness, unity, and reverence before the Lord. You can probably think of a number of items. But let's try to sum up all those qualities with one not very exciting word: *healthy*. You want a healthy family—a family that works and lives and loves together as God designed the family to do.

So it is for our churches. I propose that Christians, whether pastors or church members, should aspire to have healthy churches.

Maybe there's a better word to describe what the church should be than "healthy." After all, we're talking about the people purchased by the blood of the eternal Son, the King of kings and Lord of lords—is "healthy" the best that I can come up with? Yet I like the word *healthy* because it communicates the idea of a body that's living and growing as it should. It may have its share of problems. It's not been perfected yet. But it's on the way. It's doing what it should do because God's Word is guiding it.

I often tell my congregation that when it comes to battling sin in our lives, the difference between Christians and non-Christians is *not* that non-Christians sin whereas Christians don't. The difference is found in which sides we take in the battle. Christians take God's side against sin, whereas non-Christians take sin's side against God. In other words, a Christian will sin, but then he will turn to God and his Word and say, "Help me fight against sin." A non-Christian, even if he recognizes his sin, effectively responds, "I want my sin more than God."

A healthy church is not a church that's perfect and without sin. It has not figured everything out. Rather, it's a church that continually strives to take God's side in the battle against the ungodly desires and deceits of the world, our flesh, and the devil. It's a church that continually seeks to conform itself to God's Word.

Let me give you a more precise definition, and then we'll look at several passages of Scripture that support this definition: *A healthy church is a congregation that increasingly reflects God's character as his character has been revealed in his Word.*

So if a pastor were to ask me what kind of church I would encourage him to aspire to have, I might say, "A healthy one, one that increasingly reflects God's character as it has been revealed in his Word."

And Christian, what kind of church might I encourage you to join and serve and patiently work toward? A healthy one,

one that increasingly reflects God's character as it has been revealed in his Word.

If you were reading carefully, you noticed that I kept saying "might." I said "might" for two reasons. First, I don't want to suggest that this is the *only* way for us to describe what churches should be. Different occasions and purposes might call for different descriptions. An author might want to respond to legalism or licentiousness in churches, and so begin his description by claiming, "The most important thing our churches can be is cross-centered." I would say "amen" to that. Or an author might want to respond to the lack of Scripture in our churches, in which case he might call for Bible-centered churches. Again, I would say, "amen."

Second, I don't want to presume that someone couldn't better articulate what I'm trying to get at. This is, quite simply, the best I can presently do to explain what I believe is the central biblical goal for what we should generally aspire to in our churches—reflecting the character of God as it's been revealed in his Word.

What Christian doesn't want that?

Thoroughly Equipped

Imaging God's character as it's been revealed in his Word means, quite naturally, beginning with God's Word. Why should we turn there, and not to "whatever works" in determining what our churches should *do* and *be*? In Paul's second letter to Timothy, the pastor of the church in Ephesus, he told Timothy that the Bible would "equip him for every good work." In other words, there are no good works for which Scripture would not equip Timothy—or us. If there is something our churches think they should do or be that's *not* found in God's Word, then Paul was wrong, because in that case Scripture couldn't be said to equip us for "every good work."

Does that mean I'm saying we shouldn't use the good brains God has given us? No, I'm just saying let's start with Scripture and see what we find.

I want to look briefly at six moments in the storyline of the Bible that will help us to see that we want churches that increasingly reflect God's character as it's been revealed in his Word. The Bible does tell a story, you know. This story has countless subplots, but all these subplots participate in one grand story. Our goal here is to see if we can discern what God wants for the church in this storyline.

Image Is Everything
1) CREATION

In Genesis, God created the plants and the animals "each according to its kind" (ESV). Every apple is patterned after every other apple, and every zebra is patterned after every other zebra. About humankind, Scripture reads, "Let us make man in our image, in our likeness" (1:26). Man is not patterned after every other man. He is patterned after God. He uniquely mirrors, or resembles, God.

Given that we've been uniquely created in the image of God, humans must uniquely *image* God and God's glory before the rest of creation. Like a son who acts like his father and follows in his father's professional footsteps (Gen. 5:1ff; Luke 3:38), man is designed to *represent* God's character and rule over creation: ". . . and let them rule over the fish of the sea and the birds of the air, over the livestock, over all the earth" (Gen. 1:26).

2) FALL

But man decided not to represent God's rule. He revolted against God and went to work representing his own rule. God therefore gave man what he asked for and banished him from his presence. Man's moral guilt meant that he could no longer draw near to God on his own.

Did humans preserve the image of God in the fall? Yes, Genesis reaffirms the fact that man is still made in God's "image" (5:1; 9:6). But both image and imaging are now distorted. The mirror is bent, you might say, and so a false image is portrayed, like a grotesque carnival mirror. Even in our sin we are imaging something about God—true and false things mixed together. In the language of the theologians, man became both "guilty" and "corrupt."

3) ISRAEL

God, in his mercy, had a plan to both *save* and *use* a group of people for accomplishing his original purposes for creation—the display of his glory. He promised a man named Abram that he would bless him and his descendants. They, in turn, would be a blessing to all nations (Gen. 12:1–3). He called them a "holy nation" and a "kingdom of priests" (Ex. 19:5–7), meaning they had been specially set apart to mediate, or image, God's character and glory to the nations by obeying the law he gave them (as Adam was supposed to do). Show the world what I'm like, God was saying to Israel. "Be holy, because I am holy" (Lev. 11:44; 19:2; 20:7).

He even called this nation his "son," since sons were expected to follow in their father's footsteps (Ex. 4:22–23). And he promised to dwell together with this son in the land he was giving them, a platform on which the nation could display God's glory (1 Kings 8:41–43).

Yet God also warned this son that if he failed to be obedient and display his holy character, he would cast him out of the land. To make a long story short, the son didn't obey, and God cast him out of his presence and the land.

4) CHRIST

One of the main lessons of ancient Israel is that fallen human beings, left to themselves, cannot image God—even if they have all the advantages of God's law, God's land, and God's presence. How every one of us should be humbled by the story of Israel! Only God can image God, and only God can save us from sin and death.

So God sent his one and only divine Son to be "born in the likeness of men" (Phil. 2:7 ESV). This beloved Son, with whom the Father was well pleased, submitted himself fully to the rule, or kingdom, of God. He did what Adam did not do—resist Satan's temptation: "Man does not live on bread alone, but on every word that comes from the mouth of God," he told the tempter when fasting in the wilderness (Matt. 4:4).

And he did what Israel did not do. He lived entirely according to the Father's will and law: "I do nothing on my own but speak just what the Father has taught me" (John 8:28; see also 6:38; 12:49).

This Son who perfectly imaged his Father could say to the

disciple Philip, "Anyone who has seen me has seen the Father" (John 14:9).

Like Father, like Son.

Looking back, the writers of the New Testament epistles would refer to him as the "image of the invisible God" (Col. 1:15) and "the radiance of God's glory and the exact representation of his being" (Heb. 1:3). As the last Adam and the new Israel, Jesus Christ redeemed the image of God in man.

Yet not only did Christ image God's glorious holiness through obedience to the law; he displayed God's glorious mercy and love by dying on the cross for sinners, paying the penalty of guilt they deserved (John 17:1–3). This substitutionary sacrifice is something the Old Testament had been pointing toward all along. Think of the animals that were slain to cover the nakedness of Adam and Eve after they had sinned. Think of how God provided a ram in the thicket for Abraham and Isaac, saving Isaac. Think of Joseph, the son who was sacrificed and sent away by his brothers so that he could one day mediate for a nation. Think of the people of Israel smearing a lamb's blood over the doors of their houses, sparing Israel's firstborn sons. Think of Israelite families bringing their sin offerings to the temple courtyard, placing their hands on the head of an animal and then cutting its throat—"the blood shed by the animal should be mine." Think of the high priest entering the Holy of Holies once a year to offer a sacrifice of atonement for all the people. Think of the prophet Isaiah's promise, "He was pierced for our transgressions, he was crushed for our iniquities; the punishment that brought us peace was upon him, and by his wounds we are healed" (Isa. 53:5).

All these and much more pointed to Jesus Christ, who went to the cross as the sacrificial lamb of God. As he told his disciples in the upper room, he went to offer a "new covenant in his blood" for all who would repent and believe.

5) CHURCH

We who were dead in our sins were made alive when we were baptized into Christ's death and resurrection. So Paul declares, "You are all sons of God through faith in Christ Jesus, for all of you who were baptized into Christ have clothed yourselves with Christ" (Gal. 3:26–27). And "Because you are sons, God sent the Spirit of his Son into our hearts, the Spirit who calls out, 'Abba, Father'" (Gal. 4:6–7).

What are these many sons of God to do? We are to display the *character* and *likeness* and *image* and *glory* of the Son and the Father in heaven!

Jesus tells us to be "peacemakers," since the Father has made peace between himself and us through the sacrifice of his Son (Matt. 5:9).

Jesus tells us to "love [our] enemies," since our Father in heaven loved us, who were once his enemies (Matt. 5:45; Rom. 5:8).

Jesus tells us to "love one another," since he gave his own life to love us and since it would show the world what he is like (John 13:34–35).

Jesus prayed that we would "be one," even as he and the Father are one (John 17:20–23).

Jesus tells us to "be perfect," as our heavenly Father is perfect (Matt. 5:48).

Jesus tells us to be "fishers of men" and disciple makers in all the nations (Matt. 4:19; 28:19). He sends us just as the Father has sent him (John 20:21).

Like Father, like Son, and like sons.

Cleansed of their sin by the work of Christ, and granted new-creation, born-again hearts by the work of the Spirit, his people have begun to recover the perfect image of God. Christ is our firstfirsts (1 Cor. 15:23). He removed the veil and opened a way for the church to behold the Father's image once more (2 Cor. 3:14, 16). We behold his image by faith now, and "are being transformed into the same image from one degree of glory to another" (2 Cor. 3:18 ESV).

Do you want to see God's purpose for the church summed up in just two verses? Paul declares,

[God's] intent was that now, through the church, the manifold wisdom of God should be made known to the rulers and authorities in the heavenly realms, according to his eternal purpose which he accomplished in Christ Jesus our Lord. (Eph. 3:10–11)

How does the church display the manifold wisdom of God? Only an all-wise God could devise a way to reconcile his love and his justice while saving a sinful people who are estranged from him and from one another. And only an all-wise God could devise a way to turn hearts of stone into hearts of flesh that love and praise him. May the cosmic powers in all the universe look on and marvel.

6) GLORY

We will image him most perfectly when we see him perfectly in glory: "But we know that when he appears we shall be like him, because we shall see him as he is" (1 John 3:2 ESV). Holy like him. Loving like him. United like him. This verse isn't promising that we'll be gods. It's promising that our souls will gleam brightly with his character and glory, like perfect mirrors facing toward the sun.

Story Recap

Did you follow the story? Here's the recap. God created the world and humankind to display the glory of who he is. Adam and Eve, who were supposed to image God's character, didn't. Neither did the people of Israel. So God sent his Son to image his holy and loving character and to remove the wrath of God against the sins of the world. In Christ, God came to display God. And in Christ, God came to save.

Now the church, which has been granted the life of Christ and the power of the Holy Spirit, is called to display the character and glory of God to all the universe, testifying in word and action to his great wisdom and work of salvation.

Friend, what are you looking for in a church? Good music? A happening atmosphere? A traditional order of service? How about:

> *a group of pardoned rebels . . .*
> *whom God wants to use to display his glory . . .*
> *before all the heavenly host . . .*
> *because they tell the truth about him . . .*
> *and look increasingly just like him—holy, loving, united?*

CHAPTER FOUR

THE ULTIMATE HOW-TO GUIDE: HOW TO DISPLAY GOD'S CHARACTER

I confess I'm not very good at practical things around the house—building bookshelves, wiring a stereo system, figuring out what all the buttons do on my telephone. I don't even find most how-to guides helpful. Often I have to cast myself on the mercy and ingenuity of family members and friends.

I am grateful that my lack of skill in some of these practical areas is no impediment for following the ultimate how-to guide—what the Bible says about how the church can display God's glorious character. The basic principle here is quite simple: we must listen to God's Word, and we must follow it. Only two steps—listen and follow.

By listening and following God's Word, we image and display God's character and glory, much like a king's ambassadors.

Or like a son. Imagine a son whose father journeyed to a distant country and then wrote his son a series of letters, instructing him on how he was to carry on the family name and how he was to conduct the family business. Yet suppose that the son never read his father's letters. How would this son ever learn to represent the father and conduct the father's business? He wouldn't. And neither does the local church that ignores the Word of God.

Two Kinds of People

Ever since Adam was cast from the garden for not obeying God's Word, all of humanity has been divided between two camps: those who obey God's Word and those who don't. Noah did. The builders of Babel didn't. Abraham did. Pharaoh didn't. David did. Most of his sons didn't. Zacchaeus did. Pilate didn't. Paul did. The super-apostles didn't.

And on we can go into church history. Athanasius did. Arius didn't. Luther did. Rome didn't. Machen did. Fosdick didn't.

I certainly don't claim to have divine, infallible insight into this latter group. But biblical history *does* reliably teach us that what separates the people of God from both impostors and unbelievers is that the people of God listen to God's Word and heed it. The others don't.

This is what Moses is at such great pains to communicate in Deuteronomy as he stands on the edge of the Promised Land with the people of Israel a second time. He begins by reminding them that he had stood there forty years prior with their parents, and that their parents hadn't listened. So God cursed their parents to die in the wilderness. The three speeches, which follow through the course of almost thirty chapters, can be summed up pretty simply: "Listen. Hear. Write down. Remember what God has said. He's the one who saved you from bondage in Egypt, so listen to him!" In chapter 30,

Moses brings the weight of everything he has said to bear on this one command: "Now choose life" (v. 19).

The people of God will find life entirely and exclusively through listening to God's Word and obeying it. It's that simple.

God's message for the New Testament church is no different. He saved us from the bondage of sin and death when we listened to his Word and believed (Rom. 10:17). Now we are to listen to his Word and follow. By listening and following what he has said, we increasingly image his character and glory.

Someone might object, "That sounds inwardly focused. Isn't the church called to be outwardly focused—onto missions? Onto evangelism?" Certainly it is called to those things. That's part of displaying the character of God. "Come, follow me," Jesus said, "and I will make you fishers of men" (Matt. 4:19), or, as Jesus said elsewhere, "As the Father has sent me, I am sending you" (John 20:21). When we do missions and evangelism and the work of the kingdom, we do so in conformity with the Word of God, in this case in conformity with Matthew 4:19, John 20:21, and many more passages. We don't do these things because some theologian thought them up and because we all agree they are a good idea. We preach, evangelize, and do the work of the kingdom *because God says to do these things in his Word.*

After all, history is not principally divided between those who evangelize and those who don't. That's not *fundamentally* what defines the church. It's divided between those who listen to God and those who don't.

That's why **Matthew** reported what Jesus said to Satan

concerning man's living on "every word that comes from the mouth of God" (Matt. 4:4), as well as Jesus' final words to his disciples—to make disciples in all nations, baptizing them and "teaching them to obey everything I have commanded you" (Matt. 28:20).

That's why **Mark** reported Jesus' parable of the seed that is planted in four different soils as a parable about the Word of God (Mark 4). Some will accept it. Some won't.

That's why **Luke** described himself as an eyewitness and a servant of the Word (Luke 1:2), and why he reports Jesus' promise, "Blessed . . . are those who hear the word of God and obey it" (Luke 11:28).

That's why **John** reported Jesus' last words to Peter as the thrice-repeated "feed my sheep" (John 21:15–17). Feed them with what? The Word of God.

That's why, when the early church in **Acts** gathered, they "devoted themselves to the apostles' teaching and to the fellowship, to the breaking of bread and to prayer" (Acts 2:42).

That's why Paul told the **Romans**, "Faith comes from hearing the message, and the message is heard through the word of Christ" (Rom. 10:17).

That's why he told the **Corinthians** that the "message of the cross" is the "power of God" unto salvation (1 Cor. 1:18): for "God was pleased through the foolishness of what was preached to save those who believe" (1 Cor. 1:21). And that's why later he told the same church that he did not "peddle the word of God for profit" or "distort the word of God," but "[set] forth the truth plainly" for their eternal benefit (2 Cor. 2:17; 4:2).

That's why he told the **Galatians** that if "anybody is

preaching [to them] a gospel other than [what he preached to them] let him be eternally condemned!" (Gal. 1:9).

That's why he told the **Ephesians** that they were "included in Christ [when they] heard the word of truth, the gospel of [their] salvation" (Eph. 1:13). He also told them that God "gave some to be apostles, some to be prophets, some to be evangelists, and some to be pastors and teachers, to prepare God's people for works of service, so that the body of Christ may be built up until we all reach unity in the faith and in the knowledge of the Son of God and become mature, attaining to the whole measure of the fullness of Christ" (Eph. 4:11–13).

That's why he told the **Philippians** that, because of his chains, "most of the brothers in the Lord have been encouraged to speak the word of God more courageously and fearlessly" (Phil. 1:14).

That's why he told the **Colossians**, "Let the word of Christ dwell in you richly as you teach and admonish one another with all wisdom" (Col. 3:16).

That's why he told the **Thessalonians**, "We also thank God continually because, when you received the word of God, which you heard from us, you accepted it not as the word of men, but as it actually is, the word of God, which is at work in you who believe" (1 Thess. 2:13), and why, later on, he instructed them, "Brothers, stand firm and hold to the teachings we passed on to you, whether by word of mouth or by letter" (2 Thess. 2:15).

That's why he told his disciple **Timothy** that the elders he chose for the church must be "able to teach," while the deacons who served in his church "must keep hold of the deep truths of the faith with a clear conscience" (1 Tim. 3:2, 9). In a subsequent letter, he told Timothy that his job description was centered on one basic thing:

> Preach the Word; be prepared in season and out of season; correct, rebuke and encourage—with great patience and careful instruction. For the time will come when men will not put up with sound doctrine. Instead, to suit their own desires, they will gather around them a great number of teachers to say what their itching ears want to hear. They will turn their ears away from the truth and turn aside to myths. (2 Tim. 4:2–4)

That's why he rejoiced with **Titus** that God had "brought his word to light through the preaching entrusted to [him] by the command of God our Savior" (Titus 1:3).

That's why Paul encouraged **Philemon** to be active in sharing his "faith"—the word "faith" referring not to an emotionally subjective state but to a defined set of beliefs (Philem. 6).

That's why the author of **Hebrews** warned, "For the word of God is living and active. Sharper than any double-edged sword, it penetrates even to dividing soul and spirit, joints and marrow; it judges the thoughts and attitudes of the heart" (Heb. 4:12).

That's why **James** reminded his readers that God "chose to give us birth through the word of truth" and to "not merely listen to the word, and so deceive yourselves. Do what it says" (James 1:18, 22).

That's why **Peter** reminded the saints scattered over a number of regions that they had "been born again, not of perishable seed, but of imperishable, through the living and enduring word of God" (1 Peter 1:23), and that "the word of the Lord stands forever" (1:25). It's also why he said in a second letter, "No prophecy of Scripture came about by the prophet's own interpretation. For prophecy never had its origin in the will of man, but men spoke from God as they were carried along by the Holy Spirit" (2 Peter 1:20–21).

That's why **John** wrote, "If anyone obeys his word, God's love is truly made complete in him. This is how we know we are in him: Whoever claims to live in him must walk as Jesus did" (1 John 2:5–6); and why he said, "And this is love: that we walk in obedience to his commands" (2 John 6); and why he declared that he has "no greater joy than to hear that my children are walking in the truth" (3 John 4).

That's why **Jude** spent almost his entire letter warning his readers against false teachers (Jude 4–16), and promising that the Lord was coming to "judge everyone, and to convict all the ungodly of all the ungodly acts they have done in the ungodly way, and of all the harsh words ungodly sinners have spoken against him" (Jude 15).

And that's why John, in the book of **Revelation**, commended the church in Philadelphia, "I know that you have little strength, yet you have kept my word and have not denied my name" (Rev. 3:8).

* * *

Friend, the church finds its life as it listens to the Word of God. It finds its purpose as it lives out and displays the Word of God. The church's job is to listen and then to echo. That's it. The primary challenge churches face today is not figuring out how to be "relevant" or "strategic" or "sensitive" or even "deliberate." It's figuring out how to be faithful—how to listen, how to trust and obey.

In that sense, we're just like the people of Israel preparing to enter the Promised Land. God is saying to us, "Listen, church: follow!" The good news is that we have, unlike ethnic Israel, the full revelation of God in Jesus Christ. And we have the Spirit of his Son, the seal and promise of our redemption.

Let's Keep Listening

All this is why we want to keep listening as we get into the second half of this book. What else does God have to teach us in his Word about a healthy church? The nine marks of a healthy church we turn now to discuss are not, I hope, just my ideas. They are just my attempt to prompt *all of us* to keep listening. Look back at the table of contents and you'll see what I mean: expositional (or *biblical*) preaching, *biblical* theology, a *biblical* understanding of the good news, a *biblical* understanding of conversion, a *biblical* understanding of church membership, *biblical* church discipline, and so on.

Even if you don't agree with something I say in the following chapters, I hope you disagree because you think the Bible says something different from what I think it says. In other words, I hope you too will let your listening to his Word guide what you think the local church should be and do.

QUICK TIPS:
IF YOU'RE THINKING ABOUT
LEAVING A CHURCH . . .

Before You Decide to Leave

1. Pray.

2. Let your current pastor know about your thinking before you move to another church or make your decision to relocate to another city. Ask for his counsel.

3. Weigh your motives. Is your desire to leave because of sinful, personal conflict or disappointment? If it's because of doctrinal reasons, are these doctrinal issues significant?

4. Do everything within your power to reconcile any broken relationships.

5. Be sure to consider all the "evidences of grace" you've seen in the church's life—places where God's work is evident. If you cannot see any evidences of God's grace, you might want to examine your own heart once more (Matt. 7:3–5).

6. Be humble. Recognize you don't have all the facts and assess people and circumstances charitably (give them the benefit of the doubt).

If You Go

1. Don't divide the body.

2. Take the utmost care not to sow discontent even among your closest friends. Remember, you don't want anything to hinder their growth in grace in this church. Deny any desire to gossip (sometimes referred to as "venting" or "saying how you feel").

3. Pray for and bless the congregation and its leadership. Look for ways of doing this practically.

4. If there has been hurt, then forgive—even as you have been forgiven.

PART 2

ESSENTIAL MARKS OF A HEALTHY CHURCH

ESSENTIAL MARKS OF A HEALTHY CHURCH

We've decided we want healthy churches. We want congregations of people who increasingly reflect the character of God as it has been revealed in his Word. Let churches be big. Let them be little. Let them be urban or rural, traditional or contemporary. Let them meet in houses, buildings, schools, or storefronts. Just let them display for the world what our holy and loving God is like. May they testify to God's marvelous glory in word and deed.

The question we then have to consider is *what marks a healthy church*?

If we were talking about maintaining a healthy physical body, the conversation would turn at this point to eating a balanced diet, exercising, getting enough sleep, and so on. What about the church body?

Throughout this section and the next, I will lay out nine marks of a healthy church. These marks are not everything one would want to say about a church. They are not even necessarily the most important things about a church. For example, baptism and communion are essential aspects of a biblical church, as students of church history will tell you. Yet they are not directly discussed here. That is because virtually every church at least intends to practice them. The nine attributes discussed here are marks that may distinguish a sound, healthy, biblical church from many of its more sickly sisters. These nine marks are found too rarely today and are, therefore, in special need of being brought to our attention and cultivated in our churches.

In this section I'm going to describe what I'm calling three *essential* marks of a healthy church. The essential marks are, in every sense, essential. Take away expositional preaching, biblical theology, and a biblical understanding of the gospel, and you'll watch that church's health decline quickly and radically. In fact, expect it to expire soon (even if its doors are technically open).

Sadly, church history is littered with countless examples of pastors who, perhaps with good motives, sought to make their churches more "relevant" or "timely" by compromising one of these three marks. In a sense, they tried to be wiser than God. Friend, do not follow this path.

If a man calls me and asks whether he should accept a pastorate with a church that does not want him to preach expositionally, I will probably discourage him from accepting that position. If a Christian calls me and says that a false gospel is consistently taught from the pulpit of her church, I will likely encourage her to consider changing churches.

Why would I state this so strongly? For the same reason I would discourage someone from going to a restaurant where they don't actually serve food but serve only pictures of food. God's Word, and God's Word alone, gives life!

CHAPTER FIVE

AN ESSENTIAL MARK OF A HEALTHY CHURCH: EXPOSITIONAL PREACHING

If a healthy church is a congregation that increasingly displays the character of God as his character has been revealed in his Word, the most obvious place to begin building a healthy church is to call Christians to listen to God's Word. God's Word is the source of all life and health. It's what feeds, develops, and preserves a church's understanding of the gospel itself.

What It Is

Fundamentally, this means that both pastors and congregations must be committed to expositional preaching. Expositional preaching is the kind of preaching that, quite simply, *exposes* God's Word. It takes a particular passage of Scripture, explains that passage, and then applies the meaning of the passage to the life of the congregation. It's the kind of preaching most geared to get at what God says to his people, as well as to those who are not his people. A commitment to expositional preaching is a commitment to hear God's Word.

There are many other types of preaching. Topical preaching, for example, gathers up one or more Scriptures on a particular topic, such as the topic of prayer or the topic of giving. Biographical preaching takes the life of someone in the Bible and portrays the individual's life as a display of God's grace and as an example of hope and faithfulness. And these other types may be employed helpfully on occasion. But the regular diet of the church should consist of the explanation and application of particular portions of God's Word.

The practice of expositional preaching presumes a belief that what God says is authoritative for his people. It presumes that his people *should* hear it and *need* to hear it, lest our congregations be deprived of what God intends to use for shaping us after his image. It presumes that God intends the church to learn from both Testaments, as well as from every genre of Scripture—law, history, wisdom, prophesy, gospels, and epistles. An expositional preacher who moves straight through books of the Bible and who regularly rotates between the different Testaments and genres of Scripture, I believe, is like a mother who serves her children food from every food group, not just their two or three favorite meals.

An expositional preacher's authority begins and ends with Scripture. Even as Old Testament prophets and New Testament apostles were given not just a commission to go and speak, but to speak a particular message, so Christian preachers today have authority to speak from God so long as they speak his words.

What It Isn't

Someone may happily profess that God's Word is authoritative and that the Bible is inerrant. Yet if that person in practice (intentionally or not) does not preach expositionally, he denies his own claim.

Sometimes people confuse expositional preaching with the style of a particular expositional preacher whom they have observed. But expositional preaching is not fundamentally a matter of style. As others have observed, expositional preaching is not so much about *how a preacher says* what he says, but about *how a preacher decides* what to say. Is Scripture determining our content or is something else? Expositional preaching is not marked by a particular form or style. Styles will vary. Instead it's marked by a biblical content.

Sometimes people confuse expositional preaching with reading a verse and then preaching on a topic loosely related to that verse. Yet when a preacher exhorts a congregation on a topic of his choosing, using biblical texts only to back up his point, he will never preach more than what he already knows. And the congregation will only learn what the preacher already knows. Expositional preaching requires more than that. It requires careful attention to the context of a passage, because it aims to make the point of the biblical text the point of the sermon. When a preacher exhorts a congregation by preaching a passage of Scripture in context—where the point of the passage is the point of his sermon—both he and the congregation will end up hearing things from God that the preacher did not intend to say when he first sat down to study and prepare for the sermon ("Next week, we'll look at Luke 1, and whatever God has for us in Luke 1. The following week, we'll look at Luke 2, and whatever God has for us in Luke 2. The week after that . . .").

This should make sense as we think about every step of our Christian lives, from our initial call to repentance all the way to the Spirit's most recent work of conviction. Has not every step of growth in grace occurred when we heard from God in ways we hadn't heard from him before?

A preacher's ministry must be characterized by this very practical form of submission to the Word of God. Yet make no mistake: it is finally the congregation's responsibility to ensure that this is true of its preachers. Jesus assumes that congregations have the final responsibility for what happens in a church in Matthew 18, as does Paul in Galatians 1. A church, therefore, must never give a person spiritual oversight over the body who does not show a practical commitment to hearing and teaching God's Word. When it does, it hampers its growth, ensuring that it won't mature beyond the level of the pastor. The church will slowly be conformed to the image of the pastor, rather than to the image of God.

The Way God Has Always Worked

God's people have always been created by God's Word. From creation in Genesis 1 to the call of Abram in Genesis 12, from the vision of the valley of the dry bones in Ezekiel 37 to the coming of the living Word, Jesus Christ—God has always created his people by his Word. As Paul wrote to the Romans, "Faith comes from hearing the message, and the message is heard through the word of Christ" (Rom. 10:17). Or, as he wrote to the Corinthians, "Since in the wisdom of God the world through its wisdom did not know him, God was pleased through the foolishness of what was preached to save those who believe" (1 Cor. 1:21).

Sound, expositional preaching is often the fountainhead of true growth in a church. Martin Luther found that carefully attending to God's Word began a reformation. We, too, must commit to seeing that our churches are always being reformed by the Word of God.

Back to the Heart of Worship

During a day-long seminar on Puritanism that I taught at a church in London, I remarked at one point that Puritan sermons were sometimes two hours long. A member of the class gasped audibly and asked, "What time did that leave for worship?" Clearly, the individual assumed that listening to God's Word preached did not constitute worship. I replied that many English Protestants in former centuries believed that the most essential part of their worship was *hearing* God's Word in their own language (a freedom purchased by the blood of more than one martyr) and *responding* to it in their lives. Whether they had time to sing, though not entirely insignificant, was of comparatively little concern to them.

Our churches, too, must recover the centrality of the Word in our worship. Music is a biblically required response to God's Word, but the music God gave us was not given to build our churches upon. A church built on music—of whatever style—is a church built on shifting sands.

Christian, pray for your pastor—that he will commit himself to study Scripture rigorously, carefully, and earnestly. Pray that God will lead him to understand the Word, to apply it to his own life, and to apply it wisely to the church's life (see Luke 24:27; Acts 6:4; Eph. 6:19–20). Also, grant your pastor time during the week to prepare good sermons. Preaching is *the* fundamental component of pastoring. Then speak words of encouragement to him by telling him how the faithfulness he has shown to the Word has grown you in God's grace.

Pastor, pray these things for yourself. Pray also for other churches in your neighborhood, city, nation, and around the world that preach and teach God's Word. Finally, pray that our churches would commit to hearing God's Word preached expositionally, so that the agenda of each church will be increasingly shaped by God's agenda in Scripture. Commitment to expositional preaching is an essential mark of a healthy church.

CHAPTER SIX

AN ESSENTIAL MARK OF A HEALTHY CHURCH: BIBLICAL THEOLOGY

What do you think these italicized words mean: "But we know that when he appears, *we shall be like him*, for we shall see him as he is" (1 John 3:2).

If you carefully read through the biblical storyline presented in chapter 3, you would probably know that these words point to how, at the end of time, the church will purely reflect God's loving and holy character apart from the distorting influence of sin.

Yet if you were sitting in a Mormon tabernacle, you would hear that the words "we will be like him" mean that we will all become gods!

What's the difference between these two interpretations? One is informed by the theology of the whole Bible; the other is not.

In the last chapter we said that expository preaching is essential for the health of a church. Yet every method, however good, is open to abuse. Our churches should not only be concerned with *how* we are taught, but also with *what* we are taught. That's why a second essential mark of a healthy church is sound biblical theology, or theology that's biblical. Otherwise we will interpret individual verses to mean whatever we want them to mean.

Soundness

Soundness is an old-fashioned word. Yet we should cherish soundness—soundness in our understanding of the God of the Bible and his ways with us. Paul uses the word "sound" a number of times in his pastoral writings to Timothy and Titus. It means "reliable," "accurate," or "faithful." At root, it is an image from the medical world meaning whole or healthy. Biblically sound theology, then, is theology that is faithful to the teaching of the entire Bible. It reliably and accurately interprets the parts in terms of the whole.

In his first letter to Timothy, Paul says that "*sound* doctrine" is doctrine that "conforms to the . . . gospel" and opposes ungodliness and sin (1 Tim. 1:10–11). Later on, he contrasts "false doctrines" with "the *sound* instruction of our Lord Jesus Christ and . . . godly teaching" (1 Tim. 6:3).

In his second letter to Timothy, Paul exhorts him, "What you heard from me, keep as the pattern of *sound* teaching, with faith and love in Christ Jesus" (2 Tim. 1:13). Then he warns Timothy that "the time will come when men will not put up with *sound* doctrine. Instead, to suit their own desires, they will gather around them a great number of teachers to say what their itching ears want to hear" (2 Timothy 4:3).

When Paul writes another young pastor, Titus, he shares similar concerns. Every man Titus appoints as an elder of a

church, Paul says, "must hold firmly to the trustworthy message as it has been taught, so that he can encourage others by
sound doctrine and refute those who oppose it" (Titus 1:9).
False teachers must be rebuked "so that they will be *sound* in
the faith" (Titus 1:13). And, finally, Titus "must teach what is
in accord with *sound* doctrine" (Titus 2:1).

Pastors should teach sound doctrine—doctrine that is
reliable, accurate, and faithful to the Bible. And churches are
responsible for keeping their pastors accountable to sound
doctrine.

Unity, Diversity, and Charity

We cannot lay out here everything that constitutes sound
teaching since that would require us to reproduce the whole
Bible. But in practice, every church decides where it requires
complete agreement, where it permits limited disagreement,
and where it allows complete liberty.

In the church I serve in Washington DC, we require every
member to believe in salvation through the work of Jesus
Christ alone. We also confess the same (or very similar) understandings of believer's baptism and of church structure (that is,
who has the final say in decisions). Agreement on baptism and
structure are not essential for salvation, but they're practically
helpful and health-giving for the life of the church.

On the other hand, our church allows some disagreement
over matters that are necessary neither for salvation nor for the
practical life of the church. We all agree that Christ will return, but
there are a range of opinions about the timing of his return.

Finally, our church allows entire liberty on matters still

less central or clear, such as the rightness of armed resistance or the question of who wrote the book of Hebrews.

There's a principle running through all of this: the closer we get to the heart of our faith, the more we expect unity in our understanding of the faith—in sound biblical doctrine. The early church put it this way: in essentials, unity; in nonessentials, diversity; in all things, charity.

Complex or Controversial Doctrines

A church that is committed to sound teaching will commit to teaching the biblical doctrines churches too often neglect. To our eyes, certain doctrines may look difficult or even divisive. Yet we can trust that God has included them in his Word because they are foundational for understanding his work in salvation.

The Holy Spirit is no fool. If he has revealed something in his Book for all the world to read, churches should not think of themselves as so wise that they do better to avoid certain subjects. Should they exercise pastoral wisdom and care when speaking about some things? Surely. Should they avoid those things entirely? Surely not. If we want churches that are guided by sound doctrine from the Bible, we must come to terms with the entire Bible.

The biblical doctrine of election, for example, is often avoided as too complex or too confusing. Be that as it may, the doctrine is undeniably biblical. While we may not understand everything about election, it is no small matter that our salvation ultimately issues from God rather than from ourselves.

There are a number of important questions that the Bible answers but churches commonly neglect such as:

- Are people basically bad or good? Do they merely need encouragement and self-esteem, or do they need forgiveness and new life?
- What did Jesus Christ do by dying on the cross? Did he actually and effectively satisfy the just wrath of the Father, or did he merely set an example of self-sacrifice for his followers?
- What happens when someone becomes a Christian?
- If we are Christians, can we be sure that God will continue to care for us? If so, is his continuing care based on our faithfulness, or on his?

All these questions are not simply for bookish theologians or young seminary students. They are important for every Christian. Those of us who are pastors know how differently we would shepherd our people if our answer to any one of the above questions changed. Faithfulness to Scripture demands that we speak about these issues with clarity and authority, as does our desire to display the character of God in all its fullness.

Just consider: If we want churches that display God's character, don't we want to know everything he has revealed about himself in the Bible? What does it say about our opinion of his character if we don't?

Resisting God's Sovereignty

Our understanding of what the Bible teaches about God is crucial. The biblical God is Creator and Lord. Yet his sovereignty is sometimes denied, even within the church. When confessing Christians resist the idea of God's sovereignty in creation or salvation, they are really playing with pious paganism. Christians will have honest questions about God's sovereignty.

But a sustained, tenacious denial of God's sovereignty should concern us. To baptize such a person may be to baptize a heart that remains, in some ways, unbelieving. To admit such a person into membership may be to treat the individual as if he were trusting God when in fact he's not.

Such resistance is dangerous in any Christian, but it's even more dangerous in the leader of a congregation. When a church appoints a leader who doubts God's sovereignty or who misunderstands the Bible's teaching, that church sets up as their example a person who may be deeply unwilling to trust God. And this is bound to hinder that church's growth.

Too often today, the consumer-driven and materialistic culture around us encourages churches to understand the Spirit's work in terms of marketing and to turn evangelism into advertising. God himself is made over in the image of man. In such times, a healthy church must be especially careful to pray that its leaders would have a biblical and an experiential grasp of God's sovereignty. They should also pray that their leaders would remain fully committed to sound doctrine in its full, biblical glory. A healthy church is marked by expository preaching and by theology that's biblical.

CHAPTER SEVEN

AN ESSENTIAL MARK OF A HEALTHY CHURCH: A BIBLICAL UNDERSTANDING OF THE GOOD NEWS

It is particularly important for our churches to have sound biblical theology in one special area—in our understanding of the good news of Jesus Christ, the gospel. The gospel is the heart of Christianity, and so it should be at the heart of our churches.

A healthy church is a church in which every member, young and old, mature and immature, unites around the wonderful good news of salvation through Jesus Christ. Every text in the Bible points to it or some aspect of it. So the church gathers week after week to hear the gospel rehearsed once again. A biblical understanding of the good news should inform every sermon, every act of baptism and communion, every song, every prayer, every conversation. More than anything else in the church's life, the members of a healthy church pray and long to know this gospel more deeply.

Why? Because the hope of the gospel is the hope of know-ing the glory of God in the face of Christ (2 Cor. 4:4–6). It's the hope of seeing him clearly and knowing him fully, even as we are fully known (1 Cor. 13:8). It's the hope of becoming like him as we see him as he is (1 John 3:2).

Gospel Basics

The gospel is not the news that we're okay. It's not the news that God is love. It's not the news that Jesus wants to be our friend. It's not the news that he has a wonderful plan or pur-pose for our life. As I discussed at greater length in chapter 1, the gospel is the good news that Jesus Christ died on the cross as a sacrificial substitute for sinners and rose again, making a way for us to be reconciled to God. It's the news that the Judge will become the Father, if only we repent and believe. (Go back to chapter 1 for a fuller explanation.)

Here are four points I try to remember whenever sharing the gospel, whether in private or in public—(1) God, (2) man, (3) Christ, and (4) response. In other words:

- Have I explained that God is our holy and sovereign creator?
- Have I made it clear that we humans are a strange mixture, wonderfully made in God's image yet horribly fallen, sinful, and separated from him?
- Have I explained who Jesus is and what he has done—that he is the God-man who uniquely and exclusively stands in between God and man as a substitute and resurrected Lord?
- And finally, even if I've shared all this, have I clearly stated that a person must respond to the gospel and must believe this message and so turn from his life of self-centeredness and sin?

Sometimes, it's tempting to present some of the very real benefits of the gospel *as* the gospel itself. And these benefits tend to be things that non-Christians naturally want, like joy, peace, happiness, fulfillment, self-esteem, or love. Yet presenting them *as* the gospel is presenting a partial truth. And, as J. I. Packer says, "A half truth masquerading as the whole truth becomes a complete untruth."[1]

Fundamentally, we don't need just joy or peace or purpose. We need God, himself. Since we are condemned sinners, then, we need his forgiveness above all else. We need spiritual life. When we present the gospel less radically, we simply ask for false conversions and increasingly meaningless church membership lists, both of which make the evangelization of the world around us more difficult.

Gospel Overflow

When a church is healthy, and its members know and cherish the gospel above everything else, they will increasingly want to share it with the world. George W. Truett, a great Christian leader of the past generation and pastor of First Baptist Church in Dallas, Texas, said:

> The supreme indictment that you can bring against a church
> . . . is that such a church lacks in passion and compassion for
> human souls. A church is nothing better than an ethical club if
> its sympathies for lost souls do not overflow, and if it does not
> go out to seek to point lost souls to the knowledge of Jesus
> Christ.[2]

---

[1]Quoted in John Owen, "Introduction," in *The Death of Death in the Death of Christ* (Edinburgh: Banner of Truth, 1959, rprt. 1983), 2.
[2]George W. Truett, *A Quest for Souls* (New York: Harper & Brothers, 1917), 67.

Today, the members of our churches will spend far more time with non-Christians in their homes, offices, and neighborhoods for far longer than they will spend with other Christians—let alone non-Christians—on Sundays. Evangelism is not something we mainly do by inviting someone to church. Each of us has tremendous news of salvation in Christ. Let's not barter it for something else. Let's share it today!

A healthy church knows the gospel, and a healthy church shares it.

QUICK TIPS:
HOW TO FIND A GOOD CHURCH

1. Pray.

2. Seek counsel from a godly pastor (or from elders).

3. Keep your priorities straight.

- The gospel must be truly affirmed, clearly preached, and faithfully lived out. A serious lack in any of these expressions of the gospel is very dangerous.

- The preaching must be faithful to Scripture, personally challenging, and central to the congregation's life. You will only grow spiritually where Scripture is treated as the highest authority.

- Also very important is to consider how the church regulates baptism, the Lord's Supper, church membership, church discipline, and who has the final say in decision making.

- In short, read chapters 5 to 13 in this book!

4. Ask yourself diagnostic questions such as:

- Would I want to find a spouse who has been brought up under this church's teaching?

- What picture of Christianity will my children see in this church—something distinct or something a lot like the world?

- Would I be happy to invite non-Christians to this church? That is, would they clearly hear the gospel and see lives consistent with it? Does the church have a heart for welcoming and reaching non-Christians?

- Is this church a place where I can minister and serve?

5. Consider geography. Would the church's physical proximity to your home encourage or discourage frequent involvement and service? If you're moving to a new area, try to locate a good church home before you buy a house.

PART 3

IMPORTANT MARKS OF A HEALTHY CHURCH

IMPORTANT MARKS OF A
HEALTHY CHURCH

Insofar as all of the nine marks outlined in this book are biblical, they are authoritative for Christ's churches. Yet the distinction between the *essential* and the *important* marks should remind us that sanctification—in the church's life as in the individual's life—occurs slowly. Just as God calls us to patience in raising our children, so he calls us to patience with our churches.

What I'm calling the *important* marks are important, at least when they are considered individually, but their absence doesn't necessitate leaving a church (but it may be wise to do so). Rather, churches without these important marks can be places to pray, to be patient, and to set a good example by your own life.

If a pastor asks me how long he should endure an unbiblical leadership structure, or if a Christian asks me how long she should overlook a church's failure to practice church discipline, or if a deacon asks me how long he should bear with highly inaccurate membership roles, I very well may encourage the saint to be patient, to pray, to set a good example, to love, and to wait. Growth occurs slowly. And the church is a people—a people we are called to forgive, to encourage, to serve, to occasionally and winsomely challenge, and most of all to cherish.

Just as there are no perfect Christians in this life, so there are no perfect churches. Even the best churches fall far short of the ideal. Neither correct polity nor courageous preaching, neither sacrificial giving nor doctrinal orthodoxy, can ensure that a church will flourish. Nevertheless, any church can be healthier than it currently is. In this life, we never see complete victory over sin. But as the true children of God we do not therefore give up the struggle. Churches must not give up the struggle either. Christians, particularly pastors and church leaders, should long and labor to see healthier churches.

CHAPTER EIGHT

AN IMPORTANT MARK OF A HEALTHY CHURCH: A BIBLICAL UNDERSTANDING OF CONVERSION

At my church's first meeting back in 1878, the church adopted a statement of faith. It was a strengthened version of the 1833 New Hampshire Confession of Faith. The old language may be a bit tough, but try to press through it. Article VIII of this statement reads,

> We believe that Repentance and Faith are sacred duties, and also inseparable graces, wrought in our souls by the regenerating Spirit of God; whereby being deeply convinced of our guilt, danger and helplessness, and of the way of salvation by Christ, we turn to God with unfeigned contrition, confession, and supplication for mercy; at the same time heartily receiving the Lord Jesus Christ as our Prophet, Priest and King, and relying on Him alone as the only and all sufficient Saviour.

Not many people speak or write like this anymore. Yet the biblical truths here haven't changed. A healthy church is marked by a biblical understanding of conversion.

Our Work

The statement begins with the biblical call to repentance and faith. As Jesus commanded at the beginning of his ministry, "Repent and believe the good news!" (Mark 1:15). In the simplest terms, conversion equals repentance and faith.

As the Confession continues, it provides a further description of what repentance and faith look like. It says we "turn" to God from our sin, we "receive" Christ, and we "rely" on him alone as the all sufficient Savior. The New Testament is filled with pictures of sinners leaving their sin, receiving Christ, and relying upon him. Think of Levi the tax collector leaving his trade to follow Christ. Or the woman at the well. Or the Roman centurion. Or Peter, James, and John. Or Saul, the persecutor of Christians, turned Paul, the apostle to the Gentiles. The list is long. Each of them turns, trusts, and follows. That's conversion.

It's not reciting a creed. It's not saying a prayer. It's not a conversation. It's not becoming a Westerner. It's not reaching a certain age, attending a class, or passing through some other rite of adulthood. It's not a journey, everyone strewn along the path at different points. Rather, conversion is turning with our whole lives from self-justification to Christ's justification, from self rule to God's rule, from idol worship to God worship.

Conversion Is God's Work in Us

Yet notice what this statement also says about our conversion. We turn because we are "deeply convinced of our guilt, danger and helplessness, and of the way of salvation by Christ." How does this happen? Who convinces us? It is "wrought in our souls by the regenerating Spirit of God." The statement cites two Scriptures to support this idea:

> When they heard this, they had no further objections and praised God, saying, "So then, God has granted even the Gentiles repentance unto life." (Acts 11:18)

> It is by grace you have been saved, through faith—and this not from yourselves, it is the gift of God. (Eph. 2:8)

If we understand our conversion as something we have done, apart from what God first does in us, then we misunderstand it. Conversion certainly includes our action, as we've discussed. Yet conversion is much more than that. Scripture teaches that we must have our hearts replaced, our minds transformed, our spirits given life. We can't do any of this. The change every human needs is so radical, so much at our very root, that only God can do it. He created us the first time. So he must make us new creations. He was responsible for our natural birth. So he must give us a new birth. We need God to convert us.

The nineteenth-century preacher Charles Spurgeon once told a story of how he was walking down a London street when a drunken man approached him, leaned on the lamppost nearby, and said, "Hey, Mr. Spurgeon, I'm one of your converts!"

Spurgeon responded, "You must be one of mine—you're certainly not one of the Lord's!"

Bad Fruit and Good

When a church misunderstands the Bible's teaching on conversion, it may well become filled with people who made sincere pronouncements at one point in their lives but who have not experienced the radical change the Bible presents as conversion.

True conversion may or may not involve an emotionally heated experience. However, it *will* evidence itself in its fruit. Do lives give evidence of change—putting off the old and putting on the new? Are members interested in waging war against their sin, even if they continue to stumble? Do they show a new interest in enjoying fellowship with Christians, and perhaps new motives in spending time with non-Christians? Are they beginning to respond to trials and challenges differently from how they did as non-Christians?

A right understanding of conversion will show up not only in the sermons, but in a church's requirements for baptism and the Lord's Supper. Care will be exercised. Pastors will not be pressured to baptize people hastily and without examination.

It will show up in the church's expectations for membership. Admittance is not immediate. Perhaps a membership class is offered. A testimony is requested, as well as an explanation of the gospel from the prospective member.

It will show up in the church's unwillingness to view known sin lightly. Accountability, encouragement, and the occasional rebuke are ordinary, not extraordinary. Church discipline is practiced, as we'll consider in chapter 12.

Understanding the Bible's presentation of conversion is one of the important marks of a healthy church.

CHAPTER NINE

AN IMPORTANT MARK OF A HEALTHY CHURCH: A BIBLICAL UNDERSTANDING OF EVANGELISM

So far, we have described healthy churches as marked by expositional preaching, biblical theology, and a biblical understanding of the gospel and conversion. That means when churches don't teach the Bible and sound doctrine they become unhealthy.

What does an unhealthy church look like? It's a church where the sermons often veer into cliché and repetition. Worse yet, they become moralistic and me-centered, and the gospel is recast as little more than spiritual "self-help." Conversion is viewed as an act of human resolve. And by varying degrees, from bad to worse, the culture of the church is indistinguishable from the secular culture surrounding it.

Such congregations do not herald the tremendous news of salvation in Jesus Christ, to say the least.

Evangelism Shaped by Understanding of Conversion

As we turn to consider another important mark of a healthy church—a biblical understanding of evangelism—it's worth considering how much our view of this mark will be shaped by our understanding of the previous ones (the marks that are both *essential* and *important*), especially conversion.

On the one hand, if our minds have been shaped by what the Bible teaches about God and how he works, as well as by what it teaches about the gospel and what sinful human beings ultimately need, then a right understanding of evangelism will generally follow. We will attempt to spur on evangelism principally through teaching and meditating on the gospel itself, not through learning methods for sharing it.

I am always heartened by how new Christians seem innately aware of the gracious nature of their salvation. You may even have heard testimonies in the last few months that confess that conversion is the work of God (Eph. 2:8–9). "I was totally lost in sin, but God . . ."

On the other hand, if what the Bible says about God's work in conversion is left to the side in our churches, then evangelism becomes our doing whatever we can to produce a verbal confession. One sign that a church may not have a biblical understanding of conversion and evangelism is that its membership is markedly larger than its attendance. Such a church should stop and ask why its evangelism produces such a large number of members it never sees yet who feel secure in their salvation. What did we tell them that discipleship in Christ means? What did we teach them about God, sin, and the world?

For all members of the church, but particularly for leaders who have the responsibility of teaching, a biblical understanding of evangelism is crucial.

What Is Evangelism?

According to the Bible, Christians are called to care, to plead, and even to persuade unbelievers (2 Cor. 5:11). Yet we are to do so by "setting forth the truth plainly," which means "renouncing secret and shameful ways" (2 Cor. 4:2).

Evangelism, in other words, is not about doing everything we can to get a person to make a decision for Jesus, much less about imposing our views. Attempting to force a spiritual birth will prove to be as effective as Ezekiel trying to stitch dead, dry bones together to make a person (Ezekiel 37), or as likely as Nicodemus giving himself a new birth in the Spirit (John 3).

Furthermore, evangelism is not the same thing as sharing a personal testimony. It's not the same thing as presenting a rational defense of the faith. It's not even doing works of charity, though all three of these things may accompany evangelism. Nor should evangelism be confused with the results of evangelism, as if to say we've only successfully evangelized when a conversion follows.

No, evangelism is speaking words. It's sharing news. It's being faithful to God by presenting the good news that we discussed in chapter 8—that Christ, by his death and resurrection, has secured a way for a holy God and sinful people to be reconciled. God will produce true conversions when we present this good news (see John 1:13; Acts 18:9–10). In short, evangelism is presenting the good news freely and trusting God to convert people (see Acts 16:14). "Salvation comes from the Lord" (Jonah 2:9; cf. John 1:12–13).

How to Evangelize

When I evangelize, I attempt to convey three things to people about the decision that must be made about the gospel:

- The decision is costly, so it must be carefully considered (see Luke 9:62).
- The decision is urgent, so make it soon (see Luke 12:20).
- The decision is worth it, so you want to make it (see John 10:10).

This is the message we need to communicate personally to family and friends. This is the message we need to communicate corporately as a whole church.

There are some excellent resources in print about evangelism. For considering the close connection between our understanding of the gospel and the evangelistic methods we use, I recommend Will Metzger's *Tell the Truth* (InterVarsity Press), Iain Murray's *The Invitation System* and *Revival and Revivalism* (Banner of Truth Trust), as well as my own *The Gospel and Personal Evangelism* (Crossway, forthcoming).

Another important mark of a healthy church, then, is a biblical understanding and practice of evangelism. The only true growth is the growth that comes from God and through his people.

CHAPTER TEN

AN IMPORTANT MARK OF A HEALTHY CHURCH: A BIBLICAL UNDERSTANDING OF MEMBERSHIP

Is church membership a biblical idea? In one sense, no. Open up the New Testament, and you won't find a story about, say, Priscilla and Aquila moving to the city of Rome, checking out one church, then another, and finally deciding to join a third. From what we can tell, nobody went "church shopping" because there was only one church in each community. In that sense, you won't find a list of church members in the New Testament.

But the churches of the New Testament apparently kept lists of people, such as the lists of widows supported by the church (1 Timothy 5). More significantly, a number of passages in the New Testament suggest that churches did have some way of delineating their members. They knew who belonged to their assemblies and who did not.

On one occasion, for instance, a man in the Corinthian church was living in immorality "that does not occur even among pagans" (1 Cor. 5:1). Paul wrote the Corinthians and told them to exclude this man from their assembly. Now stop and think about this. You cannot formally *exclude* someone if he is not formally *included* in the first place.

Paul appears to refer to this same man in his subsequent letter to the Corinthians by referring to the "punishment inflicted on him by the majority" (2 Cor. 2:6). Stop and think again. You can only have a "majority" if there is a defined group of people, in this case a defined church membership.

Paul cared "who was in" and "who was out." He cared because the Lord Jesus himself had granted churches the authority to draw a line—as best as they humanly can—around themselves, to mark themselves off from the world.

> "Truly, I say to you, whatever you bind on earth shall be bound in heaven, and whatever you loose on earth shall be loosed in heaven." (Matt. 18:18 ESV; see also 16:19; John 20:23)

Healthy churches, we have said, are congregations that increasingly reflect the character of God. Therefore, we want our earthly records to approximate, as much as possible, heaven's own records—those names recorded in the Lamb's book of life (Phil. 4:3; Rev. 21:27).

A healthy church aspires to receive and to dismiss individuals professing faith, just as the New Testament authors instruct. That is, it aspires to have a biblical understanding of membership.

Biblical Membership Means Commitment

A temple has bricks. A flock has sheep. A vine has branches. And a body has members. In one sense, church membership begins when Christ saves us and makes us a member of his body. Yet his work must then be given expression in an actual local church. In that sense, church membership begins when we commit to a particular body. Being a Christian means being joined to a church.

Scripture therefore instructs us to assemble regularly so that we can regularly rejoice in our common hope and regularly spur one another on to love and good deeds (Heb. 10:23–25). Church membership is not simply a record of a box we once checked. It's not a sentimental feeling. It's not an expression of affection toward a familiar place. It's not an expression of loyalty or disloyalty toward parents. It should be the reflection of a living commitment, or it is worthless. Indeed, it's worse than worthless; it's dangerous, as we'll consider in a moment.

Biblical Membership Means Taking Responsibility

The practice of church membership among Christians occurs when Christians grasp hold of each other in responsibility and love. By identifying ourselves with a particular local church, we are telling the church's pastors and other members not just that we commit to them, but that we commit to them in gathering, giving, prayer, and service. We are telling them to expect certain things from us and to hold us accountable if we don't follow through. Joining a church is an act of saying, "I am now your responsibility, and you are my responsibility." (Yes, this is countercultural. Even more, it's counter to our sinful natures.)

Biblical membership means taking responsibility. It comes from our mutual obligations as spelled out in all of

Scripture's *one another* passages—love one another, serve one another, encourage one another. All of these commands should be encapsulated in the covenant of a healthy church (see appendix).

Getting the last three marks correct will help with getting this mark correct. Church members will grow to recognize their mutual responsibilities the more they cherish the gospel, understand that conversion is God's work, and evangelize by instructing "seekers" to count the cost. Less will Christians regard their churches with a come-as-you-please and get-what-you-can attachment—one more store to peek your head into at the Christian mall or market. More will they view them as a body in which all parts care for one another—the home in which they live.

Sadly, it is not uncommon to find a big gap between the number of people officially on the membership rolls and the number who regularly attend. Imagine a church of three thousand members with only six hundred regularly attending. I fear that many evangelical pastors today might be more proud of their so-called membership than distressed by the large number of members not attending. According to one recent study, the typical Southern Baptist church has 233 members with only 70 attending on Sunday morning.

And is our giving any better? What congregations have budgets that equal—let alone exceed—10 percent of the combined annual incomes of their members?

Physical limitations can prevent attendance and financial burdens can prevent giving. But otherwise one wonders if churches are making idols out of numbers. Numerical figures can be idolized just as easily as carved figures—perhaps more easily. Yet God will assess our lives and weigh our work, I think, rather than count our numbers.

Biblical Membership Means Salvation Affirmation

What's so dangerous about nonattending, responsibility-shirking members? Uninvolved members confuse both real members and non-Christians about what it means to be a Christian. And active members do the voluntarily inactive members no service when they allow them to remain members of the church, since membership is the church's corporate endorsement of a person's salvation. Did you catch that? By calling someone a member of your church, you are saying that that individual has your church's endorsement as a Christian.

So if a congregation has not set its eyes upon an individual for months, even years, how can it testify that that person is faithfully running the race? If an individual is missing in action but has not joined some other Bible-believing church, how do we know if he or she was ever really a part of us (see 1 John 2:19)? We don't necessarily know that such uninvolved people are not Christians; we simply can't affirm that they are. We don't have to tell the individual, "We know you're going to hell"; we only have to say, "We can no longer express our confidence that you're going to heaven." When a person is perpetually absent, a church endorsement is, at best, naïve; at worst, dishonest.

A church that practices biblical church membership does not require perfection of its members; it requires humility and honesty. It doesn't call them to bare decisions but to real discipleship. It doesn't discount the importance of an individual's own experiences with God, but neither does it assume too much of those not-yet-perfected individuals. This is why the New Testament presents a role for a corporate affirmation by those in covenant with God and with each other.

Biblical Membership Is Meaningful

I hope to see the membership statistics in churches become more and more meaningful so that the members in *name* become members in *fact*. From time to time, this means removing names from the church rolls (though not from our hearts). Most often, this means teaching new members what God intends for the church and continually reminding current members of their commitment to the life of the church. In my own church, we do this in a number of ways, from membership classes to reading the church covenant aloud every time we receive the Lord's Supper.

As our church has grown in healthiness, the head count on Sunday mornings has once again exceeded the number of names officially on our rolls. Surely this should be your desire for your church as well.

We don't love old friends well by allowing them to hold onto their membership in our congregations for sentimental reasons. We love them by encouraging them to join another church where they can love and be loved on a weekly, even daily, basis. In my own church's covenant, therefore, we pledge, "We will, when we move from this place, as soon as possible unite with some other church where we can carry out the spirit of this covenant and the principles of God's Word." This commitment is part of healthy discipleship, particularly in our transient age.

A recovered practice of careful church membership will

have many benefits. It will make the witness of our churches to non-Christians more clear. It will make it harder for weaker sheep to stray from the fold and still call themselves sheep. It will help shape and focus the discipleship of more mature Christians. It will help church leaders know exactly for whom they are responsible. In all of this, God will be glorified.

Pray that church membership will come to mean more than it currently does. That way, we can better know whom to pray for and whom to encourage and challenge in the faith. Church membership means being incorporated in practical ways into the body of Christ. It means traveling together as aliens and strangers in this world as we head to our heavenly home. Certainly another mark of a healthy church is a biblical understanding of church membership.

CHAPTER ELEVEN

AN IMPORTANT MARK OF A HEALTHY CHURCH: BIBLICAL CHURCH DISCIPLINE

Flowing directly out of a biblical understanding of church membership is biblical church discipline. *Membership* draws a boundary line around the church, marking the church off from the world. *Discipline* helps the church that lives inside of that boundary line stay true to the very things that are cause for drawing the line in the first place. It gives meaning to being a member of the church and is another important mark of a healthy church.

What exactly is church discipline? In the narrowest sense, it is the act of excluding someone who professes to be a Christian from membership in the church and participation in the Lord's Supper for serious unrepentant sin—sin they refuse to let go of.

Imaging God's Character

In order to understand church discipline, it might help us to rehearse what was said in chapter 3 about God's purposes in creating the universe, humanity, Israel, and the church. God created the universe in order to display his glory. He then created humanity for the same purpose, and particularly by creating us to bear his image (Gen. 1:27). Humanity—Adam and Eve—didn't display his glory, so he excluded them from the garden.

God then called Israel to display his glory, particularly by displaying his holiness and character to the nations as they were revealed in the law (see Lev. 19:2; Prov. 24:1, 25). Along the way, this law was the basis for correcting and even excluding some people from the community (as in Num. 15:30–31). Ultimately, it was the basis for excluding Israel itself from the land.

Finally, God created the church, we have said, so that it might increasingly reflect the character of God as it's been revealed in his Word. In keeping with the storyline of the entire Bible, then, church discipline is the act of excluding an individual who carelessly brings disrepute onto the gospel and shows no commitment to doing otherwise. Discipline helps the church to reflect God's glorious character faithfully. It helps the church to remain holy. It's an attempt to polish the mirror and remove any specks (see 2 Cor. 6:14–7:1; 13:2; 1 Tim. 6:3–5; 2 Tim. 3:1–5). Why discipline? So that the holy and loving character of God might appear more clearly and shine more brightly.

How Does It Work?

How does the process of discipline work? Since the circumstances of sin vary tremendously, so does the need for pastoral wisdom in knowing how to treat each situation particularly.

That said, Jesus' words in Matthew 18 provide the general

boundaries (Matt. 18:15–17). Begin by addressing a sinning brother or sister in private. If the sinner repents, the process of discipline ends. If not, then return a second time with another Christian. If he or she still doesn't repent, then, as Jesus put it, "tell it to the church; and if he refuses to listen even to the church, treat him as you would a pagan or a tax collector" (Matt. 18:17), that is, like an outsider.

Shalt Thou Judge?

This whole idea can sound harsh to many people today. Besides, didn't Jesus forbid his followers from judging others? In one sense, he certainly did: "Do not judge, or you too will be judged" (Matt 7:1). But in the very same Gospel, Jesus also called churches to rebuke—even publicly—their members for sin (Matt. 18:15–17; cf. Luke 17:3). So whatever Jesus meant by "Do not judge," he did not mean to rule out everything that might be called "judging" today.

Certainly God himself is a judge. He judged Adam in the garden. In the Old Testament he judged both nations and individuals. In the New Testament he promises that Christians will be judged according to their works (see 1 Corinthians 3). And he promises that, on the final day, he will reveal himself as the ultimate judge of all humanity (see Revelation 20).

In his judgment, God is never wrong. He is always righteous (see Joshua 7; Matthew 23; Luke 2; Acts 5; Romans 9). Sometimes his purposes in judgment are corrective, redemptive, and restorative, as when he disciplines his children. Sometimes his purposes are retributive, vengeful, and final, as when he bears his wrath upon the ungodly (see Hebrews 12). Either way, God's judgment is always just.

What may surprise many people today is that God occasionally uses human beings to carry out his judgment. The state is given responsibility to judge its citizens (see Romans 13). Christians are told to judge themselves (see 1 Cor. 11:28; Hebrews 4; 2 Peter 1:5). Congregations are told to occasionally even judge the members of the church—though not in the final way God judges.

In Matthew 18, 1 Corinthians 5 and 6, and elsewhere, the church is instructed to exercise judgment within itself. This judgment is for redemptive, not vengeful, purposes (Rom. 12:19). Paul told the church in Corinth to hand the adulterous man over to Satan "so that the sinful nature may be destroyed and his spirit saved" (1 Cor. 5:5). He says the same to Timothy regarding the false teachers in Ephesus (1 Tim. 1:20).

Closed or Open?

We should not be surprised that God calls us to exercise certain forms of judgment, or discipline. If churches expect to have anything to say about how Christians *do* live, they will have to say something about how Christians *do not* live. Yet I worry that the way many churches approach discipleship is like pouring water into leaking buckets—all the attention is given to what is poured in with no thought given to how it's received and kept. One sign of this tendency is the decline in the practice of church discipline in the last few generations.

One church-growth writer recently summed up his strategy on growing churches by saying, "Open the front door and close the back door." By this he means that churches should make themselves more accessible to outsiders while also doing a better job of follow-up. These are good goals. Yet I suspect that most pastors and churches today already aspire to do this, and to a fault. So let me offer what I believe is a more biblical strategy: *guard carefully the front door and open the back door.* In other words, make it more difficult to join, on the one hand, and make it easier to be excluded on the other. Remember—the path to life is narrow, not broad. Doing this, I believe, will help churches to recover their divinely intended distinction from the world.

One of the first steps in exercising discipline, therefore, is to exercise greater care in receiving new members. A church should ask every individual applying for membership what the gospel is and ask each one to give some evidence of understanding the nature of a Christ-honoring life. Member candidates will benefit from knowing what the church expects from them and the importance of commitment. If churches are more careful about recognizing and receiving new members, they will have less occasion to practice corrective church discipline later.

Doing Discipline Responsibly

Church discipline can be done badly. The New Testament teaches us not to judge others for the motives we might impute to them (see Matt. 7:1), or to judge each other about matters which are not essential (see Romans 14–15). In carrying out discipline, our attitudes must not be vindictive, but loving, demonstrating a "mercy, mixed with fear" (Jude 23). There's no denying it, church discipline is fraught with problems of wisdom and pastoral application. But we must remember that the whole Christian life is difficult and open to abuse. And our difficulties should not be used as an excuse to leave something unpracticed.

Each local church has a responsibility to judge the life and teaching of its leaders and members, particularly when either compromises the church's witness to the gospel (see Acts 17; 1 Corinthians 5; 1 Timothy 3; James 3:1; 2 Peter 3; 2 John).

Biblical church discipline is simple obedience to God and a confession that we need help. Can you imagine a world in which God never used our fellow human beings to enact his judgment, one in which parents never disciplined children, the state never punished lawbreakers, and churches never reproved their members? We would all arrive at judgment day never having felt the lash of earthly judgment and so been forewarned of the greater judgment then upon us. How merciful of God to teach us now about the irrevocable justice to come with these temporary chastisements (see Luke 12:4–5).

Here are five positive reasons for practicing corrective church discipline. It shows love for:

1) the good of the disciplined individual;
2) other Christians as they see the danger of sin;
3) the health of the church as a whole;
4) the corporate witness of the church and, therefore, non-Christians in the community;
5) and the glory of God. Our holiness should reflect God's holiness.

It should mean something to be a member of the church, not for our pride's sake, but for God's name's sake. Biblical church discipline is another important mark of a healthy church.

CHAPTER TWELVE

AN IMPORTANT MARK OF A HEALTHY CHURCH: BIBLICAL DISCIPLESHIP AND GROWTH

Another important mark of a healthy church is a pervasive concern for church growth as growth is prescribed in the Bible. That means growing members, not just numbers.

Some today think that a person can be a "baby Christian" for a whole lifetime. Growth is treated as an optional extra for zealous disciples. But growth is a sign of life. If a tree is alive, it grows. If an animal is alive, it grows. Being alive means growing, and growing means increasing and advancing, at least until death intercedes.

Paul hoped the Corinthians would grow in their faith (2 Cor. 10:15), and that the Ephesians would "grow up into him who is the Head, that is, Christ" (Eph. 4:15; cf. Col. 1:10; 2 Thess. 1:3). Peter exhorted his readers, "Like newborn babies, crave pure spiritual milk, so that by it you may grow up in your salvation" (1 Peter 2:2).

It is tempting for pastors and even some members to reduce their churches to manageable statistics of attendance, baptisms, giving, and membership. This kind of growth is tangible. Yet such statistics fall far short of the true growth that the New Testament authors describe and that God desires.

Growth in Holiness

How do we know when Christians are growing in grace? We don't ultimately know from the fact that they're excited, use lots of religious language, or have a growing knowledge of Scripture. Just because they exhibit an increased love for the church or display confidence in their own faith isn't determinative either. We can't even be sure Christians are growing because they appear to have an outward zeal for God. All these *may* be evidences of true Christian growth. At the same time, one of the most important and commonly overlooked signs of growth that *must* be observed is increasing holiness rooted in Christian self-denial (see James 2:20–24; 2 Peter 1:5–11). The church should be marked by a vital concern for this kind of increasing godliness in the lives of its members.

Neglecting holiness, like neglecting church discipline, results in hard-to-grow disciples. In churches where unholy behavior goes unchecked, disciples become confused and unclear about the life that is honoring to Christ. It's like a garden where the weeds are never pulled or good things never planted.

What Growth Does and Doesn't Look Like

The church has an obligation to be God's means of growing people in grace. Mature, holiness-seeking influences in a covenant community of believers can be tools in God's hand for growing his people. As God's people are built up and grow together in holiness and self-giving love, they should improve their ability to administer discipline and to encourage discipleship.

When you peer into the life of a church, the growth of its members can show up in all sorts of ways. Here are a few possibilities:

- Growing numbers being called to missions—"I've enjoyed sharing the gospel with my neighbors from South America. I wonder if God is calling me to . . ."
- Older members getting a fresh sense of their responsibility in evangelism and in discipling younger members—"Why don't you come over for dinner?"
- Younger members attending the funerals of older members out of love—"As a single man in my twenties, it was so good to be taken in by Mr. and Mrs. . . ."
- Increased praying in the church and more prayers centered on evangelism and ministry opportunities—"I'm starting an evangelistic Bible study at work and I'm a little nervous. Would the church pray that . . ."
- More members sharing the gospel with outsiders.
- Less reliance among members on the church's programs and more spontaneous ministry activities arising from members—"Pastor, what would you think if Sally and I organized a Christmas tea for the ladies in the church as an evangelistic opportunity?"
- Informal gatherings among church members characterized by spiritual conversation, including an apparent willingness to confess sin while simultaneously pointing to the cross—"Hey brother, I'm really struggling with . . ."
- Increased and sacrificial giving—"Honey, how can we cut fifty dollars from our monthly budget in order to support . . ."
- Increased fruits of the Spirit.

- Members making career sacrifices so that they can serve the church—"Did you hear that Chris turned down a promotion three times so that he could continue devoting himself to being an elder?"
- Husbands leading their wives sacrificially—"Honey, what are several things I can do to make you feel more loved and understood?"
- Wives submitting to their husbands—"Sweetheart, what are some things I can do today that will make your life easier?"
- Parents discipling their children in the faith—"Tonight let's pray for Christian workers in the country of . . ."
- A corporate willingness to discipline unrepentant and public sin.
- A corporate love for an unrepentant sinner shown in the pursuit of him or her before discipline is enacted—"Please! If you get this message, I would love to hear from you."

These are just a few examples of the kind of church growth for which Christians should pray and work. Will healthy churches grow in size? They often do, because they present an attractive witness to the gospel. But we should not assume they must. Sometimes God has other purposes, such as calling his people to patience. Our focus must remain on faithfulness and true spiritual growth.

And what's the cause of such growth? Expositional Bible preaching. Sound biblical theology. Gospel-centeredness. And a biblical understanding of conversion, evangelism, membership, discipline, and leadership!

But if churches are places where only the pastor's thoughts are taught, where God is questioned more than he is worshiped, where the gospel is diluted and evangelism perverted, where church membership is made meaningless, and a worldly cult of personality is allowed to grow up around the pastor, then one can hardly expect to find a community that is either cohesive or edifying. Such a church will not glorify God.

God Glorified By Growth

When we do encounter a church composed of members growing in Christ-likeness, who gets the glory? God does, because, as Paul said, "God made it grow. So neither he who plants nor he who waters is anything, but only God, who makes things grow" (1 Cor. 3:6b–7; cf. Col. 2:19).

Likewise, Peter concludes his second letter to a group of early Christians, "Grow in the grace and knowledge of our Lord and Savior Jesus Christ. To him be glory both now and forever! Amen" (2 Peter 3:18). We might think that our growth will bring glory to ourselves. But Peter knew better: "Live such good lives among the pagans that, though they accuse you of doing wrong, they may see your good deeds and glorify God on the day he visits us" (1 Peter 2:12). Peter obviously remembered Jesus' words: "Let your light shine before men, that they may see your good deeds *and praise you?*" No! "*. . . and praise your Father in heaven*" (Matt. 5:16). Working to promote Christian discipleship and growth is another mark of a healthy church.

CHAPTER THIRTEEN

AN IMPORTANT MARK OF A HEALTHY CHURCH: BIBLICAL CHURCH LEADERSHIP

What kind of leadership does a healthy church have? Is it a congregation that strives to ensure that the gospel is faithfully preached? Yes (Galatians 1). Is it deacons who model service in the affairs of the church? Yes (Acts 6). Is it a pastor who is faithful in preaching the Word of God? Yes (2 Timothy 4). But the Bible presents one more leadership gift to churches to help them become healthy: the position of elder.

Surely there are many useful things we could say about church leadership from the Bible; yet I want to focus primarily on this question of elders, since I fear a lot of churches don't know what they're missing. As a pastor, I pray that Christ will place within our fellowships men whose spiritual gifts and pastoral concern indicate that God has called them to be elders. May he prepare many such men!

If God has so gifted a certain man in the church with exemplary character, pastoral wisdom, and gifts of teaching, and if, after prayer, the church recognizes these things, then he should be set apart as an elder.

What Is an Elder?

In Acts 6, the young church in Jerusalem began to bicker over how food was being distributed to widows. The apostles therefore called upon the church to select several men who could better oversee this distribution. The apostles chose to delegate this particular task so that they could then "give [their] attention to prayer and the ministry of the word" (Acts 6:4).

That, in the briefest terms, appears to be the division of labor between elders and deacons that the rest of the New Testament develops. Elders are especially devoted to prayer and the ministry of the Word for the church while deacons help to sustain the church's physical operations.

Are you beginning to see what a gift this is to you, churches? God is essentially saying, "I'm going to take several men from among you and set them aside to pray for you and to teach you about me."

Elders and Congregations

All churches have had individuals designated to perform the functions of elders, even if those individuals are called by other titles, such as deacon or director. The three New Testament titles for this office, which are used interchangeably, are *episcopos* (overseer or bishop), *presbuteros* (elder), and *poimain* (shepherd or pastor). All three are used for the same men, for instance, in Acts 20:17 and 20:28.

When evangelicals hear the word "elder," however, many of them immediately think "Presbyterian." Yet the first Congregationalists (capital C, pointing to a formal group of churches) back in the sixteenth century taught that eldership was an office for New Testament churches. Elders could also be found in Baptist churches in America throughout the eighteenth and into the nineteenth century. In fact, the first president of the Southern Baptist Convention, W. B. Johnson, wrote a treatise in 1846 calling Baptist churches to use a plurality of elders since the practice was biblical.

Baptists and Presbyterians do disagree in two areas concerning elders (and I think the issues at play here are relevant to those who are not Baptist or Presbyterian). First and most fundamentally, we who are Baptists are congregationalists (lowercase *c*, referring to a practice). We believe that the Bible teaches that the final decision on matters rests with the congregation as a whole, not with a church's elders or anyone outside the church body. When Jesus was teaching his disciples about confronting a sinful brother, he said that the congregation was the final court of appeal, not the elders, not a bishop or pope, not a council or convention (Matt. 18:17). When the apostles sought out several men to act as deacons, as we just discussed, they gave the decision over to the congregation.

In Paul's letters, too, the congregation appears to assume final responsibility. In 1 Corinthians 5, Paul blames not the pastor, elders, or deacons for tolerating a man's sin, but the congregation. In 2 Corinthians 2, Paul refers to what a majority of them had done in disciplining an erring member. In Galatians 1, Paul calls on the congregations themselves to judge the false teaching they had been hearing. In 2 Timothy 4, Paul reproves not just the false teachers but also those who paid them to teach what their itching ears wanted to hear. Elders lead, but they do so, biblically and necessarily, within the bounds recognized by the congregation. In that sense, elders and every other board or committee in a Baptist church act in what is finally an advisory capacity to the whole congregation.

Second, Baptists and Presbyterians have disagreed over the roles and responsibilities of elders, largely due to different understandings of the following words written by Paul for Timothy: "The elders who direct the affairs of the church well are worthy of double honor, especially those whose work is preaching and teaching" (1 Tim. 5:17). Presbyterians understand this verse to be establishing two classes of elders—ruling elders and teaching elders. Baptists don't recognize this formal division but understand the verse to suggest that certain individuals among a group of elders will simply be given more fully, as a practical matter, to preaching and teaching. After all, Paul clearly tells Timothy earlier in the letter that a basic qualification of every elder is that he is "able to teach" (1 Tim. 3:2; see also, Titus 1:9). Baptists, therefore, have often denied the appropriateness of appointing elders who are not capable of teaching Scripture.

Plurality of Elders

Where Baptists and Presbyterians often agreed in the eighteenth century was that there should be a plurality (or multiple number) of elders in each local church. The New Testament never suggests a specific number of elders for a particular congregation, but it clearly and consistently refers to the "elders" of a local church in the plural (for example, Acts 14:23; 16:4; 20:17; 21:18; Titus 1:5; James 5:14).

Today, not only are more and more Baptist churches rediscovering this, but also churches from many other denomi-

nations, as well as independent churches, are increasingly recognizing this basic biblical idea.

A plurality of elders does not mean that the pastor has
no distinctive role. There are many references in the New
Testament to preaching and preachers that would not apply to
all the elders in a congregation. In Corinth, for instance, Paul
gave himself exclusively to preaching in a way that lay elders in
a church could not (Acts 18:5; 1 Cor. 9:14; 1 Tim. 4:13; 5:17).
Also, preachers seemed to relocate to an area for the express
purpose of preaching (Rom. 10:14–15), whereas elders seemed
settled among the community (Titus 1:5).

As the regular voice that proclaims God's Word, a faithful
preacher will probably find that a congregation and the other
elders treat him as the first among equals and "especially" worthy of double honor (1 Tim. 5:17). Still, the preacher or pastor
is, fundamentally, just one more elder, formally equal with every
other man called by the congregation to act in this capacity.

Benefits of Elders

My own experience as a pastor has confirmed the usefulness
of following the New Testament practice of sharing, wherever
possible, the responsibility for pastoring a local church with
other men rooted in the congregation.

Decisions involving the church but not requiring the attention of all the members should fall not to the pastor alone, but
to the elders as a whole. This is sometimes cumbersome, but it
has immense benefits. It rounds out the pastor's gifts, making
up for some of his defects and supplementing his judgment.
It creates support in the congregation for decisions, helping
unity and leaving leaders less exposed to unjust criticism. It

makes leadership more rooted and permanent and allows for more mature continuity. It encourages the church to take more responsibility for its spirituality and helps make the church less dependent on its employees.

This practice of a plurality of elders is unusual among Baptist churches today, but there is a growing trend toward it among Baptists and many others—and for good reason. It was needed in New Testament churches, and it is needed now.

What about Deacons?

Many modern churches tend to confuse elders with either the church staff or the deacons. Deacons also fill a New Testament office, one rooted in Acts 6, as we saw. While any absolute distinction between the two offices is difficult, deacons are generally concerned with the practical details of church life: administration, maintenance, and the care of church members with physical needs. In many churches today, the deacons have either taken over the role of spiritual oversight or they have left it entirely in the hands of one man, the pastor. It would benefit churches to again distinguish the roles of elders and deacons. Do churches not need both types of servants?

Shouldering the Burden and Privilege

Eldership is the biblical office that I hold as a pastor—I am the main preaching elder. But I work together with a group of elders for the edification of the church. Some are on staff but the majority are not. We meet regularly to pray, to talk, and to form recommendations for the deacons or the whole church. It's difficult to put into words how much these men have loved both me and our entire congregation by sharing the burden—and privilege—of pastoring. I thank God regularly for these fellow workers.

Clearly, eldership is a biblical idea that has practical value. If implemented in our churches, it could help pastors immensely by removing weight from their shoulders and even removing their own petty tyrannies from their churches. Furthermore, the character qualities listed by Paul for eldership, aside from the ability to teach, are qualities every Christian should work toward (1 Timothy 3; Titus 1). Publicly affirming certain individuals as exemplary, then, helps to present a model for other Christians, especially Christian men. Indeed, the practice of recognizing godly, discerning, trusted laymen as elders is another mark of a healthy church.

CONCLUSION:
WHERE THE RUBBER MEETS
THE ROAD

I have wanted to leave this church many times . . . all the talk about battling sin and serving others; people keeping me accountable—people who are sinful themselves." An elder in my church recently said all this.

He continued, "But I realize this is exactly the point because I'm still sinful, and I want to be done with sin. I need the accountability, the modeling, the care, the love, the attention. My flesh hates it all! But apart from all this, I probably would have divorced my wife, and then a second, and then a third, and never lived with my children. God shows his grace and care for me through his church."

Healthy churches, churches that increasingly reflect the character of God as it's been revealed in his Word, are not always the easiest places to be. The sermons might be long. The expectations might be high. The talk of sin will probably feel overdone to many. The fellowship might even feel, at least sometimes, intrusive. But the key is that word *increasingly*. If we *increasingly* reflect God's character, then it stands to reason that aspects of our lives, individually and corporately, don't reflect his character—there must be smudges on the mirror that need to be polished out, curves in the glass that need to be flattened. That takes work.

And God in his goodness has called us to live out the Christian life together, as our mutual love and care reflect the love and care of God. Relationships imply commitment in the world. Surely they imply no less in the church. He never meant our growth to occur alone on an island but with and through one another.

Does a healthy church, then, know joy? Oh, it knows joy, indeed! It knows the joy of real change. It knows the joy of broken shackles. It knows the joy of meaningful fellowship and true unity, not unity for its own sake, but unity around a common salvation and worship. It knows the joy of Christ-like love given and received. Most wonderfully, it knows the joy of "reflecting the Lord's glory" and "being transformed into his likeness with ever-increasing glory" (2 Cor. 3:18).

In the third commandment (Exod. 20:7; Deut. 5:11), God warned his people not to take his name in vain. He didn't mean to simply prohibit profane language. He also meant to warn us against taking his name upon ourselves in vain, such that our lives speak falsely about him. This command is for us as the church.

Many churches today are sick. We mistake selfish gain for spiritual growth. We mistake mere emotion for true worship. We treasure worldly acceptance rather than divine approval, an approval which is generally given to a life that is incurring worldly opposition. Regardless of their statistical profiles, too many churches today seem unconcerned about the very biblical marks that should distinguish a vital, growing church.

The health of the church should concern all Christians,

particularly those who are called to be leaders in the church. Our churches are to display God and his glorious gospel to his creation. We are to bring him glory by our lives together. This burden of display is our awesome responsibility and tremendous privilege.

So let's go back to where we started. What are you looking for in a church? Are you looking for one that reflects the values of you and your community or one that reflects the out-of-this-world and glorious character of God? Of these two options, which will better present a light on the hill for a world lost in darkness?

To Learn More . . .

For a fuller discussion of each of the nine marks, see the full-length book *Nine Marks of a Healthy Church* (Crossway, 2004). For a more practical treatment on building a healthy church, see *The Deliberate Church*, written by Paul Alexander and me. For further discussion on the structure of a church, specifically membership, elders, deacons, and congregationalism, see *A Display of God's Glory* (9Marks, 2001). Finally, you may enjoy any number of articles, audio sermons, books, and e-tutorials on church life together at www.9marks.org.

A NOTE TO THE PEW

If you have been encouraged by any of the content in this book, take care in how you propose change to your pastors. Pray, serve, encourage, set a good example in your own life, and be patient. A healthy church is less about a *place* that looks a certain way, and more about a *people* who love in the right way. And love is generally best shown when it's given in the face of circumstances we don't like. Just think, Christian, of how we have been loved in Christ!

A NOTE TO THE PASTOR

If you have been encouraged by any of the content in this book, take care in how you introduce change to your church. Be patient, love people, and preach the Word.

APPENDIX:
A TYPICAL COVENANT OF A HEALTHY CHURCH

Having, as we trust, been brought by Divine Grace to repent and believe in the Lord Jesus Christ and to give up ourselves to Him, and having been baptized upon our profession of faith, in the name of the Father and of the Son and of the Holy Spirit, we do now, relying on His gracious aid, solemnly and joyfully renew our covenant with each other.

We will work and pray for the unity of the Spirit in the bond of peace.

We will walk together in brotherly love, as becomes the members of a Christian Church; exercise an affectionate care and watchfulness over each other and faithfully admonish and entreat one another as occasion may require.

We will not forsake the assembling of ourselves together, nor neglect to pray for ourselves and others.

We will endeavor to bring up such as may at any time be under our care, in the nurture and admonition of the Lord, and by a pure and loving example to seek the salvation of our family and friends.

We will rejoice at each other's happiness, and endeavor

with tenderness and sympathy to bear each other's burdens and sorrows.

We will seek, by Divine aid, to live carefully in the world, denying ungodliness and worldly lusts, and remembering that, as we have been voluntarily buried by baptism and raised again from the symbolic grave, so there is on us a special obligation now to lead a new and holy life.

We will work together for the continuance of a faithful evangelical ministry in this church, as we sustain its worship, ordinances, discipline, and doctrines. We will contribute cheerfully and regularly to the support of the ministry, the expenses of the church, the relief of the poor, and the spread of the gospel through all nations.

We will, when we move from this place, as soon as possible, unite with some other church where we can carry out the spirit of this covenant and the principles of God's Word.

May the grace of the Lord Jesus Christ, and the love of God, and the fellowship of the Holy Spirit be with us all. Amen.

SPECIAL THANKS

While many people have helped me understand and experience what a healthy church is, two have particularly made a contribution to this book.

Matt Schmucker first suggested I turn a series of church newsletter articles into the original booklet, which this book replaces. He has consistently been an encouragement to making the thoughts in this book more widely available. Without him, I'm not sure this book would ever have come into existence.

Jonathan Leeman has had such a large hand in this book that we wondered if it wouldn't be better to put on the cover, "by Mark Dever and Jonathan Leeman." At the end of the day, the amount of material that was mine, its identification with the previous 9 Marks booklet, and the way it is written ("I" referring to me, with illustrations from my life) decided me in favor of leaving the attribution in my name. Having said that, Jonathan wrote the parable of Mr. Nose and the Hands, the long list of New Testament expressions about the use of the Word of God, and other parts of the first half of the book. He has done a superb job reorganizing and editing the old booklet into this new, enlarged—and, we hope, more useful—format. He is a talented brother from whom I am again deriving great help. And you are getting more than you know from him.

9Marks

Building Healthy Churches

9Marks exists to equip church leaders with a biblical vision and practical resources for displaying God's glory to the nations through healthy churches.

To that end, we want to see churches characterized by these nine marks of health:

1   Expositional Preaching
2   Biblical Theology
3   A Biblical Understanding of the Gospel
4   A Biblical Understanding of Conversion
5   A Biblical Understanding of Evangelism
6   Biblical Church Membership
7   Biblical Church Discipline
8   Biblical Discipleship
9   Biblical Church Leadership

Find all our Crossway titles
and other resources at
www.9Marks.org